Assassin on Stage

Assassin on Stage

Brutus, Hamlet, and the Death of Lincoln

ALBERT FURTWANGLER

University of Illinois Press

Urbana & Chicago

© 1991 by the Board of Trustees of the University of Illinois
Manufactured in the United States of America
C 5 4 3 2 1

This book is printed on acid-free paper.

Library of Congress Cataloging-in-Publication Data

Furtwangler, Albert, 1942-
    Assassin on stage : Brutus, Hamlet, and the death of Lincoln /
Albert Furtwangler.
        p.   cm.
    Includes index.
    ISBN 0-252-01746-3 (alk. paper)
    1. Shakespeare, William, 1564-1616 — Stage history — 1800-1950.
2. Brutus, Marcus Junius, 85?-42 B.C., in fiction, drama, poetry,
etc.   3. United States — History — Civil War, 1861-1865 — Literature
and the war.   4. Shakespeare, William, 1564-1616.   Julius Caesar.
5. Political plays, English — History and criticism.   6. Lincoln,
Abraham, 1809-1865 — Assassination.   7. Shakespeare, William,
1564-1616.   Hamlet.   8. Booth, John Wilkes, 1838-1865.
9. Assassination in literature.   10. Booth, Edwin, 1833-1893.
11. Tragedy.   I. Title.
PR3112.F87   1991
822.3'3 — dc20   90-38627
                                                              CIP

Contents

Illustrations follow page 30.

Preface

*O*N NOVEMBER 25, 1864, the three actor sons of the famous tragedian Junius Brutus Booth performed together in New York. Edwin Booth appeared as Brutus, Junius Brutus Booth, Jr., as Cassius, and John Wilkes Booth as Mark Antony in *Julius Caesar*, a one-night benefit performance to raise money for a statue of Shakespeare in Central Park. This was the first time the three brothers acted together; it was destined to be the last. Junius Brutus, Jr., went on to other engagements. Edwin stayed in New York. The next night he opened in *Hamlet* in a run so successful that his theater manager kept it on the boards for one hundred nights, a new record. Thereafter Edwin Booth in *Hamlet* became an American institution: Booth *was* Hamlet to thousands of admiring, even worshiping playgoers over the next quarter-century. His famous New York run ended in late March 1865, and he moved on to Boston. But meanwhile his brother John Wilkes had made his way to Washington and into his conspiracies against Abraham Lincoln. On April 9, Lee surrendered to Grant at Appomattox and the Civil War seemed all but over. Then came Good Friday, April 14, Lincoln at Ford's Theatre, a sudden shot, Booth leaping from the balcony and limping across the stage into the night and into history.

These two developments — Edwin Booth as Hamlet, his brother as Lincoln's assassin — have been studied as completely distinct chapters in theatrical and political history. Or they have been linked casually and apologetically. Booth the assassin has been explained as a failed actor, making his histrionic move in Ford's Theatre at least in part because he had proved hopeless on other stages. Or his deed has been traced back to theatrical posturings as Brutus against Caesar. Likewise, Edwin Booth's Hamlet has been seen as enriched by the actor's own personal sorrows, not least of which was the shame and grief his brother brought upon his family. Or Edwin has been admired as a noble survivor, gaining widespread honor and public affection through the steadfast practice of his art along with a blameless and generous personal life after the shock of his brother's perfidy.

But these two careers are much more intricately united. They are shaped, first of all, by the penetrating imagination of Shakespearean tragedy. *Julius Caesar* and *Hamlet* are not only plays that Shakespeare wrote about a year apart, at the beginning of his series of great tragedies. Both are also profound meditations on the art of political murder. Very specifically, they both trace the actions of a deeply conscientious and philosophical man as he steels himself to kill a powerful tyrant, arranges for public acknowledgment of his deed, and faces its personal consequences. Here as nowhere else in his drama Shakespeare ponders the psychology, the necessity, and the futility of patriotic assassination. He provides the most elaborate script we have for the most subtle of actors, or killers.

The Booths' stories are also pinned together in the wrenching era of the American Civil War. Together these brothers embodied a continuity of proud older ways, of traditions handed down from father to son, of civilized understandings of classical literature and republican government. They appeared in *Julius Caesar*, for example, as heirs of a long tradition, billed as "sons of the great Booth . . . who have come forward with cheerful alacrity to do honor to the immortal bard from whose works the genius of their father caught inspiration." But their acting was broken right there by shouts and fire bells just outside the theater. A hotel in the same building had been set ablaze, one of a dozen fires set in New York that November night. Urban guerrillas were at work; if they had fulfilled their plans they would have set fire to thirty-two buildings and reduced the city core to ruins. On stage, the upheavals of Rome were unfolding in stately speeches; right next to the stage, another upheaval was erupting with noises and alarms that could not be ignored. It is almost as if each brother heard a different cue in that same auditorium—and went on to further one kind of political drama, deafening himself to the other. And looming over both actors, binding them even closer, is the legendary Lincoln who arose from martyrdom the following April. He looms above Shakespeare's heroes as well. In one aspect, Lincoln was to become *the* tragic figure in American history. His violent death, just at the point of humane reconciliation after military victory, exactly fits the patterns of classical drama. It could not have been scripted better. For generations Lincoln was to grow in stature, as the melancholy great good man. He became the rival in living memories of the Hamlet that Edwin Booth was impersonating on stage. But in another aspect Lincoln has come to symbolize something quite contrary to tragic patterning. His life and death both bear the indelible human stains of humble, shabby, everyday American commonality. With the single shot of his pistol, John Wilkes Booth blasted not only Lincoln's skull but also our old ways of thinking about high statesmanship and high dramatic heroism.

To explore these themes in detail I here set in the foreground the careers of these two Booth brothers. I have tried to understand and explain what they would have considered their greatest roles. For each of them, it was the preparation and execution — the best word for it is reenactment — of the deliberate, conscientious, dramatic murder of a tyrant. In the background I have sketched what seems to me essential about Shakespeare's first great tragedies and Lincoln's words and deeds. The contrast between the Booths thus points to an ampler understanding of the English master of human action and the American ideal of human freedom. Lincoln's death both illustrates Shakespeare's wisdom and challenges it. More than a century after 1865 I have tried to unfold its enduring dramatic significance and power.

I have come to this study from two different kinds of academic experience. As a professor of English in Canada I teach undergraduate survey courses to students with unspecialized backgrounds and interests. But my research over the past twenty years has been a very different matter. It has led me from eighteenth-century essay series in England to complex political and constitutional debates in early America. For my teaching, I have had to rediscover and explain some recurring ideas about tragedy; in order to write two earlier books, I have had to concentrate on varied and even clashing understandings of what constitutes a fundamental law. The events of April 1865 are often discussed as a tragedy, and often used as a focus for a hiatus in the American Constitution. Once I began to look at them I became fascinated; one kind of study kept overlapping another through curious coincidences between politics and stage history. In the end I have had to narrate a deed, not interpret a text. But to recapture that deed, its historical texture, and its consciously plotted symbolism, I have had to reread Shakespeare and reread the Constitution, as well. To retell that event, I have had to balance history and literature against one another. And for reasons that will quickly become evident, I have worked to retell a familiar tale in accessible terms — that is, in language that might induce ordinary citizens to reconsider both *Julius Caesar* and the American Civil War.

Many people and resources at Mount Allison University have supported this work. For research expenses I have depended on locally administered grants from the Faculty Research Fund and the Social Science and Humanities Research Council of Canada. The Ralph Pickard Bell Library has proved rich in holdings I had not explored before; and Anne Ward has once again given me expert and efficient help in obtaining other works from far away. To prepare the final draft on word-processing equipment, I have had to rely on the skill and good nature of Robin Hamilton. Carol Gordon has given my reading of Catullus the benefit of her better understanding of Latin. And for arguing about tragedy with me through the course of an entire year, I must thank the seven alert and tenacious students of English 4350 in 1988-89: Neil Brennan, Colleen Crawley, Norman Furber, Craig Jollymore, Paul Poole, Ardith Taylor, and Jane Wells.

Several other people and institutions have also given very friendly support. The Harvard Theatre Collection; the Folger Shakespeare Library; the Hampden-Booth Library at The Players in New York, especially its librarian Raymond Wemmlinger; the Vassar College Library; the Library of Congress; and the public library of Washington, D.C., have all helped me find and study obscure holdings. Daniel J. Watermeier of the University of Toledo answered several questions by mail and followed up with futher leads. Frank Hebblethwaite at the Ford's Theatre National Historical Site prepared answers to questions I sent him in advance, opened his library and files for my use, and discussed several ideas with me. Arthur Kincaid sent a copy of conference proceedings about John Wilkes Booth as soon as they were available.

My son Tom has reawakened my pleasure in Shakespearean performance through his exploits with the Rep Company at the Taft School. And I would like to record that Benjamin DeMott first breathed life into Shakespeare's Brutus for me, when he taught English 26 at Amherst College many years ago.

While I have been writing three academic books, my wife has published four volumes of fiction. She has not given direct help to my writing, but her wonderful companionship has been a steady force in all my work.

Abbreviations

In citing works in the text and the notes, the following abbreviations have been used for works frequently cited:

EYB   Asia Booth Clarke. *The Elder and the Younger Booth.*

HEB   Charles H. Shattuck. *The Hamlet of Edwin Booth.* Urbana: University of Illinois Press, 1969.

LCW   *The Collected Works of Abraham Lincoln,* ed. Roy Basler. New Brunswick, N.J.: Rutgers University Press, 1953.

Spencer *Shakespeare's Plutarch,* ed. T. J. B. Spencer. Harmondsworth, Eng.: Penguin, 1964.

UB   Asia Booth Clarke. *The Unlocked Book: A Memoir of John Wilkes Booth.* 1938; rpt. New York: Arno, 1977.

1

The American Tragedy

*B*EFORE DISCUSSING Lincoln's death as a tragedy, it would be convenient to have a clear and precise understanding of that term. But for many reasons tragedy is a very hard term to pin down, especially when it is applied to a great public event. Part of the problem is that tragedy is a matter of feeling; and perhaps from an early age we recognize Lincoln's death as tragic without the bother of defining terms and sorting through critical categories. We may also feel uneasy about defining tragedy and thus jamming together two separate compartments of experience. The term comes from the theater, from works of patterned action on stage. And so its use may seem artificial — theatrical or stagy, and hence false — if we apply it too narrowly to events in history or life. On the other hand, we risk the vagueness of cliché if we use tragedy loosely to refer to any disaster or calamity, on any scale: if we want to distinguish Lincoln's death as tragic, we have to ask how it differs in kind from the calamity of the Civil War or the shocking loss involved in any war or any sudden death. Finally, there is the fact that even in the theater the idea of tragedy has had a varied career. We must turn to the theater to grasp the large and complex meaning of this term. But we may rightly suspect that the modern theater does not comprehend all that tragedy has been, and cannot convey the deepest sense of tragedy that older societies may have known.

1

The effect of a tragedy in the modern theater is not single, and it takes an effort to imagine that it ever was. A classic dramatist like Shakespeare or Sophocles may have done his best to arrange scenes and actions with economy, coherence, and subtle and unmistakable emphases, but his work always falls short of controlling what a modern audience feels or perceives. The fault does not lie with the intermediaries of the theater — the actors, directors, producers, or technicians. It arises from the fact that every night's audience is now a different many-headed monster. Tragedy is no longer a unifying public ritual, as it may have been in earlier centuries. For most theatergoers it is an occasional experience, a special night out. And for theater managers it has long been a regular business, the work of bringing together a succession of full houses, whose members will disperse once the curtain falls and go on to their separate lives and other entertainments. Modern, mundane distractions probably cloud the attention of many spectators. Even those who come ready to concentrate on the stage are sure to see it in a thousand different ways, changing from moment to moment. The playbill may specify *Hamlet*, date, time, and dramatis personae, but in fact innumerable dramas will take place throughout the theater simultaneously. A fine modern production will make the most of these conditions — stirring such deep memories of history, reading, playgoing, and personal experience among individual spectators as to provide matter for conversation or reflection days or weeks afterward.

Still, there is a deeper significance we recognize in the term tragedy, a special seriousness that reaches beyond entertainment and beyond the spiritual elevation of, say, a brilliant concert, even one that holds an audience together in rapt silence. We often think of tragedy as a pattern in life, which the stage serves to imitate and hold steady before us. In his *Anatomy of Criticism*, Northrop Frye provides the helpful phrase "epiphany of law" to explain this core experience. An epiphany is a supernatural revelation; but law is not supernatural in a sense determined by any particular religion. As Frye explains, law is rather "that which is and must be." This useful phrase thus suggests that tragedy takes place in the space between mystery and science, wonder and order, and forces us to see both sides of these balances at once. To perceive a tragedy is to encounter and recognize a dangerous and unchangeable power in the universe and catch at least a glimpse of its logic or coherence.

The plot of a tragedy in the theater usually unfolds a revelation of law through a long, heavy turn of cosmic irony. A single character stands out from the others around him (most tragic heroes are men); he is a hero who has already displayed extraordinary qualities. He may be notably courageous like Macbeth or Othello, or clever and forceful, like Oedipus, or simply durable and incorrigible like Lear. But a new circumstance confronts him and his people, and the hero asserts his greatest strengths of character to meet it. As a result he brings a calamity upon himself and many others. This is ironic in the sense that he achieves something quite different from what he had intended. But it is also ironic in a much richer sense. Like all irony, it reveals limitations in a character's understanding of what he is saying or doing. This is cosmic irony because it is the law or power of the universe—imagined as a god or fate or fortune or the inexorable way life works—which finally shows up the finite, helpless mortality of even the most excellent human being. Yet this experience serves to enlarge the hero's strength and humanity. He may see as profoundly as anyone can. By the end of the drama he will be dead or irreversibly maimed; he must pay that heavy a price for his decisive actions. But he may also come to a recognition of his own frailty. He will express or practice a new serenity or magnanimity or sense of horror quite unlike the virile power that carried him headlong into disaster.

The art of tragic drama lies in presenting such a profound change in a strong character—making it intelligible, convincing, and publicly acceptable—all in the course of two or three hours. Tragedy intensifies all the ordinary problems of making good theater; in fact, it stretches them to the limit.

It may seem obvious, for example, that a play should be intelligible. After all, the actors and sets are clearly visible on stage, and most scripts call for one distinct speaker at a time. But the representation of character is not the same as the presentation of costumed people saying this and doing that. The presupposition of tragedy is that the hero's character is not obvious but deep, not to be discerned in a short period of casual observation. A tragic playwright is therefore driven to develop characters with the support of the audience's prepared memory. Many dramatic characters can be worked up immediately before our eyes. But most great tragic heroes are figures from myth, legend, history, or at least some other play or story that is already widely known. From the beginning we observe and measure this version of this hero, to notice exactly how he carries an identity we already recognize. A tragic playwright also designs his work for repeated performances. It must be intelligible in the way that the music of a symphony is—attractive and coherent enough in broad outline that people will return again and again to take in its finer shadings.

It may also seem odd to stress that a tragedy should be convincing. We quickly cast aside any work of literature that purports to be serious but is evidently sloppy or contrived. Tragedy, however, faces two enormous and inescapable special problems. One is how to make the supernatural palpable. If the hero is caught in a cosmic irony, then cosmic workings must be felt on stage not as eerie lights and the rumble of drums but as dreadful realities. For a credulous audience the problem may be how to tame the supernatural so as to confine its effects to the purposes of the plot. But for a skeptical theater the hero must make credible the searing experience of meeting eye to eye with a ghost, a demon, or a band of witches or furies, or of sensing the step-by-step approach of an invisible power. The second inherent problem is how to show a change of character that is radical without being discontinuous. There must be glimmers of compassion and justice even in Oedipus's drive to torture Tiresias. We must be aware that Lear banishes Cordelia in a paralysis of rage caused by his own inexpressible love. Whatever heroic character enfolds in the last act must be visible from the first, though it later hangs forever in a new balance, like a badly jangled mobile.

The hardest task may be to make tragedy publicly acceptable. This point will hardly occur to anyone buying high-priced tickets to a classic; but the working playwright has to satisfy two grim masters, the Box Office and the Censor. The first insists that the play appeal strongly and immediately to the widest variety of playgoers. The second tacitly or directly rules out its most sensational features. Again, tragedy raises special problems in this regard. A hero's suffering offers splendid opportunities for theatrical excitement, including erotic or sadistic violence, merciless depictions of the frailties of the great, and bitter outcries against the injustice of the gods. But regimes of every stripe have found ways to suppress precisely such public exhibitions — as violations of common decency, necessary social order, or established religion. This may be one reason why high tragedies are few, and concentrated in times and places such as Shakespeare's England or fifth-century Athens, where stable, powerful regimes could foster or withstand deep questioning about ultimate powers and authorities.

A positive way of stating this point is that tragedies represent rare and precious occasions of self-scrutiny shared by a large public. They reflect not only the individual genius of the authors who wrote them but a high-minded attentiveness from the societies that encouraged them. This is not to say that tragedies have been or should be morally effective in high places, impressing their authors' deep and lasting truths on the minds and hearts of the powerful. It rather seems that the greatest tragedies have come into being when the powerful were already curious and reflective; when a theatrical tradition could develop, and more than one tragedian could refine upon the achievements of his predecessors; when a wide public could share a number of plays as common knowledge.

Two significant features of full-blown tragedy may stem from these latter conditions. One is that an audience could share a sense of reinforced civic identity. If ancient tragedy was part of a public festival, involving all citizens high and low, then the low could surely see that the high were also in attendance. If Shakespeare's plays were performed both at court and at the Globe, then the humblest playgoer would know he was witnessing the same acting company in the same play that entertained royalty. Such public countenancing of tragedy by the great may seem nugatory, until one weighs the effect of its absence. If the emperor would rather be fighting as a gladiator in the stadium; if the monarch would rather be fondling the actresses; if commanders and cabinet ministers all find their complete entertainment in athletic events, video movies, and spy novels, then there are consequences to be felt in both politics and the theater. The one will lack a revealing mirror for its magistrates, the other will have its choicest seats filled by vulgar usurpers. Plays may go on, tragedies may continue to be written, but under the strained recognition that they are reaching an incomplete public.

The other feature of tragedy at its height is that it puts an entire society on stage. Like epic, it centers on a hero who embodies the peculiar strengths and aspirations of his people. His excellence is a measure of their excellence; his downfall is an earthshaking experience for them, too. But unlike epic, tragedy does not usually focus on an ancestral hero or one whose deeds still color the world of the audience. Orestes comes for final relief to the Areopagus in Athens, but his tragic scene is Argos and the house of Atreus. King Lear calls upon courtiers with familiar English titles like Gloucester and Kent, but he is a king from ancient legend not definite history. Almost all the familiar tragic roles belong to figures from long ago and far away. This distance permits an audience to witness a story that is massive yet complete. It enables high and low, gathered in a common theater, to measure their lives against the highest strivings of another complete people with their gods.

To sum up, we might define tragedy broadly as a vision of a strong soul encountering the adversity of cosmic powers and recognizing its own unalterable limitations, and either seeing into the workings of law, or enabling us to see into them. But this understanding of tragedy is linked to the sense that it is properly expressed or embodied in the theater, that it is incomplete unless it is both dramatic and thoroughly public. It must be accessible to common apprehension, without footnotes or tedious explanations. It must be witnessed and shared by a gathering of alert yet distant spectators, who are habituated to this sort of aristocratic entertainment. And its audience must include living aristocrats, who bear witness quite visibly that the play is the thing wherein to catch the conscience of a king. The action on stage is the death or maiming of a hero. And that fact, too, underscores how public tragedy must be. The play ritualizes and makes publicly intelligible the inevitable fall of the mighty, as well as the common mystery of death. The tragic hero, however, is not merely some powerful but foredoomed mortal, ignorant, fallible, and unpredictable, who may die of a random cause at any moment. He is rather an artificial being with uncanny capacities for self-awareness. He embodies a noble society. He is the one good man who consciously acts out his people's strengths and aspirations. As a result, his death must be a fitting end of a magnificent life; it seals the end of an era.

These reflections differ, to be sure, from many accounts of tragedy that have long been respected, elaborated, debated, and fruitfully applied to particular great plays of many eras. The stress here upon practical, social dimensions in tragedy, and the idea of a common measure—the epiphany of law—unavoidably sets these pages apart from many other works that stress quite different features: Aristotelian catharsis, for example, or other psychological effects an audience should or must feel; a character's tragic flaws or mistakes or misjudgments; refinements and unities of form dear to the minds and arts of neoclassicists; and the rhythms, whether conscious or unconscious, of particular ancient rituals and legends. These suggestions may also seem wide of the mark to many critics and artists who now put their faith in the possibilities of tragedy in ordinary private life, or in the sufficiency of print or film to represent it for individual readers or spectators in the modern world.

But I have ventured to draw out this definition and trace its ramifications in the theater, in order to sharpen tragedy as a term for a unique event in American history. I believe that the social and dramatic dimensions of tragedy offer a deeper way of understanding the death of Lincoln. The details of April 1865 are in many ways thoroughly known, the perennial topic of schoolyard palaver and familiar quotation. Yet in curious ways they crisscross the features of dramatic tragedy. In some respects, they repel such patterning. In fact they bring out a sharp disparity between many cherished ideals of American politics and some central elements of tragedy as we have discussed it here.

These problems can be briefly explained here before they receive more extensive discussion in the chapters that follow.

Lincoln is certainly the most renowned and conspicuous American exemplar of the dying hero. His well-known life story recapitulates the plot of cosmic irony that we traced a moment ago. It begins with his rise to eminence by his own merits and his embodiment of traits and values that smack of the American frontier: honesty, drive, physical endurance, practical sagacity, rough humor to match an ungainly and homely exterior, kindliness and respect toward the humblest fellow laborer. With the crises of the late 1850s over slavery and westward settlement, Lincoln put forth these strengths and more, to defend the integrity of the free American Union. And thereby he brought on years of colossal suffering.

After 1861 the ironies are many and intertwined. By gaining the presidency, this defender of the Union provoked the secession of several states. By standing firm to his constitutional duties, he unleashed a bitter and protracted civil war, as well as some extraordinary violations of civil liberties. By persisting in uncompromising warfare, he oversaw the embittering devastation of a whole region he hoped to preserve. He freed slaves, but only by attaining an unprecedented concentration of despotic power. And at last he tasted victory, and the hope of reconciliation, only to fall to an assassin's bullet a week after Appomattox. Again and again the impersonal forces of a constitutional collapse revealed how limited free institutions were for governing a continental nation. And Lincoln as president became the foremost victim of conditions beyond anyone's control. Yet through the years of his presidency he seemed to ripen in wisdom. Luminous speeches and state papers that could have come only from his pen grew more and more magnanimous up to the time of his death, culminating in the Second Inaugural Address with its promises of a peaceful and generous reintegration of all the states, "with malice toward none, with charity for all."

Here, certainly, is the pattern of high tragedy: the isolation of a unique good man, his immolation in a catastrophe he helped initiate, and his survival in deeds and utterances that remain incomparably noble. What is more, here is a vision of an American hero encountering a law beyond law. The breakdown of the Constitution in a Civil War left Lincoln isolated on the public stage, and forced him to reach deep into American experience.

We still look to his words for the continuities of democracy, equality, and freedom that have sustained a divided and a reintegrated nation. The Gettysburg Address, for example, has the numinous power not only of its rhythm and imagery, but also of its occasion. It is an oracular call to rededication in the presence of near-defeat and death, from the battlefield where the Confederate forces had made their deepest invasion of the North.

And yet it is not hard to explain why Lincoln cannot remain stably fixed in our minds as a purely tragic figure. He is too immediate. His speeches and actions are too definite in the public record for any poet to reshape them. They are already known word for word and almost minute by minute. And preserved along with them are tons of commonplace memorabilia, the boots and buttons, photographs and routine documents, newspaper clippings and hearsay anecdotes that fill museums and archives. These materials do not undermine Lincoln's heroism but they do serve to diffuse it into channels of civic pride, antiquarian lore, and dusty sentimentality.

But if gray factuality thus controls the legendary Lincoln and, as it were, induces his awkward exit at stage left, a more flamboyant factuality immediately reappears to draw him back before the tragic proscenium at stage right. For Lincoln was shot in Ford's Theatre. He slumped in his chair while attending a play, so that the actors there were probably the last people he saw and heard. He was assassinated by an actor, and not merely an idle bit player but a well-known star, one of a family of celebrated tragedians. And after firing his shot, Booth quickly leapt down to the stage, held up his weapons, and cried out, "Sic semper tyrannis!" to the audience before making his escape. It was largely improvisational, to be sure, but Booth's role as assassin was wrung for a full dramatic effect.

And that role had its own tragic aspects, too. In leaping to the stage, Booth broke his leg and so helped bring upon himself his eventual capture and destruction. And in killing Lincoln he brought on consequences quite different from his apparent aims. He did not expose and destroy a malignant dictator, but sealed the martyrdom of a liberal saint. He did not strike a telling blow for the Confederacy; instead he armed its fiercest enemies with new grounds for vindictiveness. He did not even stir up much admiration for his daring; he is usually remembered as one reckless or slightly deranged young fool, who got what he deserved from the pistol of another.

Behind Lincoln and Booth there loomed further tragic shadows. Booth had aspired to be a great actor. His father and brothers had distinguished themselves on the American stage, particularly in Shakespeare. And a Shakespearean language was to touch many accounts of the assassination. The press would call Booth a Brutus. Booth's own papers would show that he thought of himself as a Brutus. Family records would merge with popular speculation to suggest that here was a frustrated actor confusing art with life, bewildering himself and tearing the world apart by attempting to do in public what he could not do in his career.

But Booth-as-Brutus is a figure of wider suggestiveness. For Brutus is Shakespeare's first portrayal of a tragically self-conscious murderer. Students of Shakespeare recognize at once that this character sums up problems that fascinated Shakespeare throughout his career and in almost all his plays. These are great political problems, problems of just rule in a world of violence and chance. What makes a ruler legitimate? What consequences to man and realm befall when a just ruler is overthrown? How can such treason be forgiven or expiated or healed? And what of unjust rulers? How are they to be withstood or controlled or purged by a society? From the first sketches of *Henry VI* to the last act of *The Tempest*, these questions continually play through Shakespeare's mind. He does not come to definitive or doctrinaire conclusions. His work as a dramatist leads him instead to reformulate these questions, setting them in new lights as he explores the particular configurations of dozens of stories. *Julius Caesar* marks a new departure after years of exploring the issues of usurpation and civil war in English history. Here Shakespeare turns to Roman history and to Brutus as the highly conscious, moral authority directing the murder of a tyrant. Shakespeare thus begins his movement away from historical pageant toward high tragedy. The next step was to be the creation of Hamlet, a tyrannicide hero of the deepest complexity.

And thereby hangs a tale. For the name Booth was to rise from the ignominy of Lincoln's assassin to new heights of fame, as John Wilkes's brother Edwin became the renowned and beloved Hamlet of nineteenth-century America.

The Lincoln assassination therefore touches lines of tragic possibility stretching backward through Elizabethan England to the foundations of ancient Rome. To see it clearly means taking these backgrounds into account. It also means weighing a curious overlapping or intersection of politics, history, and literature. In a sense, Shakespeare wrote the tragedy of Lincoln long before it occurred, and Caesar and Brutus performed it centuries before Shakespeare. Perhaps it is only through Shakespeare and Caesar that Lincoln's dimensions can be rightly appreciated, or only through our feelings about Lincoln and Booth that North Americans can gain a glimpse of tragedy in its full political power.

Problems in comprehending Lincoln's death also stretch forward in time. This is not merely because other American political heroes have been suddenly eliminated by gunfire. It is rather that the transfiguration of Lincoln from a controversial president to a hero of tragic dimensions has cast a long shadow over his successors. His legend has impressed on American politics a pattern by which statesmen should be measured or remembered, what we might call the paradigm of the tragic presidency.

Its plot runs something like this. A man of incisive mind and great gifts of language comes into office by a sudden collapse in the fortunes of his opponent's party. His term witnesses the eruption of warfare on a scale unimaginable to his predecessors. The president calls up new resources in himself and in the nation to face this enormous emergency. After protracted struggle and sacrifice he leads the nation to victory. Meanwhile he manages to inspire and unify his fellow citizens by relating the cause at hand to the most fundamental values of American life, the creeds expressed or implied in the Declaration of Independence and the Constitution. Then, just as a new, just, and lasting peace is about to be established, the president himself falls victim to a sudden calamity. He dies or is incapacitated. His power soon falls into the hands of a man notably smaller if not downright shabby by comparison. His ideals give way to compromises and scandals, while his memorable phrases linger to embarrass a generation of lackluster politicians.

This outline would fit Lincoln. But it also has a scary familiarity when set against what most of us learn as twentieth-century history. It fits Woodrow Wilson, who rose as a scholarly world leader in the Great War only to fall a cripple while campaigning for the League of Nations — and handed on his office to the cronies of Warren Harding. It fits Franklin Roosevelt, who died just as Allied victory in Europe was assured — and left Harry Truman to drop the first atomic weapons and cope with the beginnings of the Cold War. It nearly fits John F. Kennedy, who could claim moral victories in nuclear confrontations over Cuba and in active integration of southern schools but left to Lyndon Johnson the gall of Vietnam and the wormwood of racial explosions in the North.

Of course history does not simply fall into a single pattern and repeat itself. American history is much more complicated than the foregoing paragraph would suggest. Most of its coincidental features can be reasonably explained: any postwar president is bound to look smaller than a wartime commander-in-chief; sedentary men over sixty (like Wilson and Roosevelt) are vulnerable to debilitating collapse if they are kept on long and strenuous duty; many presidents have been shot at. And examined year by year or month by month, every presidential term unfolds as a welter of accomplishments and setbacks, of problems that prove intractable for decades, as well as opportunities and crises that unexpectedly occur. It is only in retrospect that a president's career can fall into a pattern, and that pattern will likely emerge out of broad comparisons with the careers of his predecessors. Presidents during great wars are bound to be measured against one another. And the ultimate modern predecessor is Lincoln.

The legend of Lincoln has therefore remained a troubling measure of greatness. It comprises concentrated military power, a rhetoric of high idealism, and a sudden shock that renders the heroic president beyond reproach for whatever ensues from his fall. By an obvious extrapolation, the paradigm of the tragic presidency encourages ever larger risks of war, entailing ever more self-righteous propaganda, and ending in the commander's glorious martyrdom. At least it reinforces a popular campaign notion that presidents should be heroes, that once in a generation there will come a man who can explain how to make the world safe for democracy or who can lead a rendezvous with destiny. This is certainly not the only measure of American or even presidential excellence, as one can readily recall by looking at the careers of the first presidents. George Washington was a military hero and a statesman anxious to leave a legacy of high ideals (witness his painstaking effort to put forth an elaborate Farewell Address). But he also made a point of leaving office peacefully for a comfortable private life. John Adams and Thomas Jefferson lived on into late old age after completing very long terms in diplomacy and public office. For James Madison, commanding a war was an embarrassment after years spent in the development of a stable constitution. It was not until Lincoln that a president was assassinated, let alone cut down at the climax of a national emergency. Whatever Lincoln himself tried to shape as his legacy to America, his career was jolted into a different pattern by the hand of John Wilkes Booth. And the results are still with us.

Booth's arrival at Ford's Theatre and his climb toward the gallery and the presidential box therefore deserve our patient study. His every step toward the back of Lincoln's head had been rehearsed already twenty centuries before he took it, and brilliantly dramatized in the Shakespearean tradition that gave him his identity and opened the guarded doors and aisles before him. Young, headstrong, probably intoxicated, certainly intent on the dangers of the moment, he cannot have imagined the full weight of the role he was performing. But we must imagine it fully if we are to transcend both its drama and its violence.

2

Brutus

*T*HE ASSASSINATION of Julius Caesar in 44 B.C. was a legendary deed long before Shakespeare reconstructed it as a tragedy. From the moment it took place, it caught the imagination of the ancient world. It was an act to shake an empire and transform its principal characters so that what they had been before that moment cannot now be recaptured. The killing was public and very dramatic, a sudden and surprising attack by a band of senators, which brought down the Roman consul with a flash of knives and the spilling of much red blood. And its aftermath was dramatic, too: in Rome, elaborate funeral orations and ceremonies, followed by riots and tumults; throughout the ancient world, slow but steady readjustments of power that eventually forced the killers into battles that ended their lives. Here certainly was an enormous eruption and discontinuity of civil order, a violent breakdown of authority at the heart of the civilized world—a historical moment that demanded an "epiphany of law."

But how is that scene to be framed? The question has vexed historians through the centuries. Did legitimacy and true Roman order end with Caesar or with Brutus? Or was their conflict but a symptom of deeper rhythms of law and history? The answers have long lain buried, beyond any definite grasp, if only because that moment itself is not recorded in ways that can satisfy a modern hunger for detail. No original documents or bits of evidence survive: no conspiratorial letters, no daggers, no blood-stained togas. The ancient historians to whom we turn had to work with traditions and records now lost. There is no way of going behind their accounts to specify exactly how much was hearsay, how much was eye-witness testimony (accurate or not), how much was official propaganda or retrospective embellishment. Appian, Plutarch, Suetonius, and Tacitus were themselves all born long after Augustus had established the Roman Empire. Their reports are therefore shaded by their own circumstances in a different political climate.

They could not, of course, disguise what everyone knew. The sudden death of Caesar remained one of the most famous and momentous events of the ancient world. It was common knowledge for centuries wherever Latin was read and Roman institutions persisted in common life. Although it could be interpreted several ways, the essential story could be told in few words.

On the Ides of March, or March 15, 44 B.C., a group of well-known Romans surrounded Caesar as he presided over the Roman senate. These men included several distinguished officials: Marcus Junius Brutus, who was praetor or civil magistrate that year; Gaius Cassius Longinus, an older general who was also a praetor; Publius Servilius Casca, who had been named a tribune for the coming year; and many others. Beginning with Casca, these men stabbed Caesar one by one and killed him. But once the deed was done, they proved inadequate to shape its outcome. Many senators were shocked by this murder in their midst. Other public officers, including the consul Marcus Antonius, refused to accept the killers' claims that they had destroyed a public enemy. Mark Antony exercised control over the city and helped stir up riots after Caesar's funeral. Within a few months the leaders Brutus and Cassius had been forced into official posts far to the east of Rome.

Meanwhile Octavian, the young grandnephew of Julius Caesar, came to Rome and began to develop astonishing powers for mastering the sit-uation. It was revealed that Caesar had adopted him and named him as his heir, and he quickly proved himself to be fully competent for that role. Soon he, Antony, and another general, Marcus Amelius Lepidus, agreed to share full power over the Roman government and quell all opposition by force. In 42 they successfully overcame the powers Brutus and Cassius had gathered at Philippi in Macedonia, and both those leaders killed themselves rather than be captured. Later, Octavian (who assumed the name Caesar Augustus) began a steady consolidation of power in his own hands. He overcame all opponents or rivals, and defeated Mark Antony at the battle of Actium in 27. During his long reign he reorganized the government of Rome. He retained power as sole emperor and left to a long succession of emperors a domain that was peaceful, rich, and firmly governed, and that extended all round the shores of the Mediterranean Sea.

Perhaps the first way of interpreting this event was that Brutus and his companions committed a cruel and shocking murder. This was certainly the attitude that justified Octavian and Mark Antony in pursuing Brutus and Cassius to their deaths. Plutarch's *Life of Julius Caesar* describes the bloody hacking of a defenseless man by a gang impervious to his pleas. Here is the scene in the translation Shakespeare read:

> So, Caesar coming into the house, all the Senate stood up on their feet to do him honour. Then part of Brutus' company and confederates stood round about Caesar's chair, and part of them also came towards him, as though they made suit with Metellus Cimber, to call home his brother again from banishment; and thus, prosecuting still their suit, they followed Caesar till he was set in his chair; who denying their petitions and being offended with them one after another, because the more they were denied, the more they pressed upon him and were the earnester with him. Metellus at length, taking his gown with both his hands, pulled it over his neck, which was the sign given the confederates to set upon him.
>
> Then Casca behind him strake him in the neck with his sword. Howbeit the wound was not great nor mortal, because, it seemed, the fear of such a devilish attempt did amaze him and take his strength from him, that he killed him not at the first blow. But, Caesar, turning straight unto him, caught hold of his sword and held it hard; and they both cried out, Caesar in Latin: "O vile traitor Casca, what doest thou?" And Casca in Greek to his brother: "Brother, help me." At the beginning of this stir, they that were present, not knowing of the conspiracy, were so amazed with the horrible sight they saw, they had no power to fly, neither to help him, not so much as once to make any outcry. They on the other side that had conspired his death compassed him in on every side with their swords drawn in their hands, that Caesar turned him nowhere but he was stricken at by some, and still had naked swords in his face, and was hacked and mangled among them, as a wild beast taken of hunters. For it was agreed among them that every man should give him a wound, because all their parts should be in this murder. And then Brutus himself gave him one wound about his privities.

Men report also that Caesar did still defend himself against the rest, running every way with his body. But when he saw Brutus with his sword drawn in his hand, then he pulled his gown over his head and made no more resistance, and was driven, either casually or purposely by the counsel of the conspirators, against the base whereupon Pompey's image stood, which ran all of the gore-blood till he was slain.[1]

A different source, the historian Suetonius, leaves the further impression that the heartless assassins left the body like trash. "All the conspirators made off, and he lay there lifeless for some time, until finally three common slaves put him on a litter and carried him home, with one arm hanging down."[2] The ancients agree that Caesar was stabbed twenty-three times, and Suetonius implies that he must have suffered, since in a physician's opinion only one of the wounds was mortal. Plutarch and Appian note that the slashing daggers cut the murderers themselves. Shakespeare amplifies this idea by having them stoop and bathe their arms in Caesar's blood.

And this gruesome crime was compounded by other wickedness. It was the murder of a great and good man. It was an act of betrayal by men he had trusted and befriended. And it unleashed a term of anarchy, destroying hundreds of other lives.

To many, Julius Caesar seemed the savior of Rome. He had established peace after years of civil war. As a general he had enlarged the realm of Roman domination, secured disputed territories, and brought new well-being to the citizens. It was true that he had become a military dictator. But his titles were duly granted by the senate in a time of crisis, and he labored to avoid outright violations of established political conventions within Rome. He was the established ruler, and his murder was viewed as an outrage against civil order — especially during the centuries of empire in Rome and of monarchy throughout Europe.

Besides, Caesar could be characterized as personally kind and indulgent, especially toward the men who attacked him. Brutus and Cassius had served Caesar's enemy Pompey, but Caesar had shown conspicuous mercy to them and had looked after their well-being. He had seen to their election as praetors and named them to other high offices in the coming year. Their treason was therefore personal as well as political. Dante was to memorialize their ingratitude by placing them along with Judas Iscariot in the mouths of a triple-faced Satan in the very bottom pit of Hell. And the legend of Caesar's death was to turn on his rueful recognition that

Brutus, even Brutus, had turned against him. "Et tu, Brute" seems to have been a tag line well before Shakespeare used it. It derives from a hearsay tradition that Brutus was Caesar's illegitimate son, the offspring of widely known intrigues with his mother Servilia. "He was stabbed with three and twenty wounds," Suetonius reports, "uttering not a word, but merely a groan at the first stroke, though some have written that when Marcus Brutus rushed at him, he said in Greek, 'You too, my child?' " (p. 111).

Finally, their deed led to uncontrolled Roman bloodshed. Within the city riots broke out and mobs tore into the innocent as well as the guilty. Shakespeare, following Plutarch, shows Caesar's mild friend, the poet Cinna, surrounded by a surly crowd. His protests do no good when they confuse him with another Cinna who was part of the conspiracy: "Tear him for his bad verses! Tear him for his bad verses!" This is but a hint of larger mayhem. Antony, Octavian, and Lepidus soon traded friends and close relatives in a ruthless purge. And for speaking out against Mark Antony the great Cicero was hunted down, killed, and publicly displayed. His head and right hand were hung on the rostrum of the Forum.

But against all these indictments for outrageous murder, Brutus and Cassius asserted a different strong line of interpretation. They were patriots, they claimed, not murderers but republican defenders of Rome against a tyrant. History has regarded Brutus in particular as the most conscientious, worthy, and effective person ever to confront and overthrow a massive dictator.

The assassins' case against Caesar was that step by step he had managed to subvert Roman institutions and make himself all-powerful. He had made his famous refusals of a kingly crown. But that was merely good politics while he in fact exercised full control over civil and military life. If there was a public emergency that made him the necessary first citizen, it was largely the result of his own actions. He had brought his army into Italy across the Rubicon in 49 to drive out Pompey and foment civil warfare from Spain to Egypt. In the period just before the assassination, he had accepted not only emergency powers as dictator but a full grant of power as dictator for life. Recently he had used his power to punish tribunes for removing crowns from his statues — even though tribunes were legally immune from such reprisals. On the day of his assassination the senate was prepared to authorize and equip him for an expedition against the Parthians. Against such barbarians he would have been entitled to lead his forces under the title of king of Rome, as long as he remained outside Italy. There was a technical limitation here, but the conspirators

saw plain implications. Unless they struck, Caesar would have taken the
ultimate step in making Rome his alone. It was true that he had no
children and so could not establish a dynasty; but as events proved, he
had named an heir, Octavian, who was capable of doing just that. And
he did have a son by Cleopatra, whom he had brought back with him
from Egypt and set up in Rome.

These are the well-known charges and suspicions that the Romans could
lay against Caesar. And in Brutus they found a noble champion. It might
almost seem he was born to bring Caesar down. The Brutus of actual life
was far from a paragon of virtues. He appears to have been cunning and
ruthless in some of his dealings, particularly in profiteering from public
office in his earlier years. But his faults could be bleached white by
comparison to the darkness of Caesar's designs. And Brutus was a man of
distinguished associations. He came of noble family, he was a learned man
himself, and he was closely linked to other conspicuous moral intellectuals
in politics.

The name Brutus was itself a potent reminder of republican ways.
Marcus Brutus traced his paternal lineage back to Lucius Junius Brutus,
one of the founders of Rome. The legend ran that he had feigned idiocy
to escape certain death from his uncle, the king Tarquinus Superbus. *Brutus*
in Latin means both "heavy" and "stupid." But when Tarquin's son raped
Lucretia, Brutus threw off his pretense and led a band of sworn followers
in an uprising that expelled the Tarquin kings. Thereafter Brutus was one
of the first two consuls, who checked each other's power, and he even
put his own sons to death when they conspired to restore the monarchy.
There are foreshadowings here of the feigned madness of Hamlet, and
Shakespeare's early poem, *The Rape of Lucrece*, is based on this story
explicitly. But the legend of this older Brutus also had its own dramatic
life; John Howard Payne's *Brutus; or, The Fall of Tarquin* (developed from
many earlier plays) was part of the Booths' standard repertory in the
nineteenth century. In any case, the younger Brutus had a history of
resistance to tyranny as close as his own name. It is on that note that
Plutarch opens the story of his life: "Marcus Brutus came of that Junius
Brutus for whom the ancient Romans made his statue of brass to be set
up in the Capitol with the images of the kings, holding a naked sword
in his hand, because he had valiantly put down the Tarquins from their
kingdom of Rome" (Spencer, p. 102).

On his mother's side the younger Brutus came from equally stern stuff.
His mother was also a descendant of a tyrannicide — the legendary Gaius

Servilius Ahala who had killed a would-be tyrant. More immediately, Servilia was the older half-sister to Cato, the severe conscience of the senate in his time. Cato, who had served as the young Brutus's guardian and mentor, later opposed Caesar to the death. He sided with Pompey and later held out with a small remnant of the senate in North Africa. When Caesar besieged them in Utica in 46, Cato fell on his sword as a martyr of the republican cause.

Soon afterward Brutus divorced his wife Claudia and suddenly married an older woman, Cato's daughter Portia (or Porcia). She was the widow of Bibulus, who had been consul with Caesar in 59 and had been squeezed out of power by him. Plutarch presents Portia as a strong-minded Stoic herself, who deliberately gashed her own thigh to prove to her husband her fearless determination. Shakespeare enlarges the point to make her an equal partner in Brutus's fortunes, the one woman who has any part in the conspiracy.

> I grant I am a woman; but withal
> A woman that Lord Brutus took to wife.
> I grant I am a woman; but withal
> A woman well reputed, Cato's daughter.
> Think you I am no stronger than my sex,
> Being so father'd and so husbanded?
> Tell me your counsels, I will not disclose 'em.
> I have made strong proof of my constancy,
> Giving myself a voluntary wound
> Here, in the thigh; can I bear that with patience,
> And not my husband's secrets?[3]

If Portia was so fathered and so husbanded, Brutus was so ancestored, so uncled, and so wived. It hardly seems that he should have had to think about assassinating Caesar; it was almost a task to which he was destined from birth. Yet he figures in history as a deliberating intellectual, the scrupulous leader who lent dignity to the assassins and restrained them from excess. He overruled the murder of Mark Antony on principle— and so left free a powerful force that would crush them all. Plutarch describes the usual contrast between Brutus and the others, naming Cassius as the ruthless plotter who drew him in as a respectable figurehead.

But [unlike the ancestral Brutus] this Marcus Brutus in contrary manner, whose *Life* we presently write, having framed his manners of life by the rules of virtue and study of philosophy, and having employed his wit, which was gentle and constant, in attempting of

great things, methinks he was rightly made and framed unto virtue.
So that his very enemies which wish him most hurt, because of his
conspiracy against Julius Caesar, if there were any noble attempt done
in all this conspiracy, they refer it wholly unto Brutus, and all the
cruel and violent acts unto Cassius, who was Brutus' familiar friend
but not so well given and conditioned as he.

(Spencer, p. 102)

Plutarch cites Mark Antony's view that Brutus alone slew Caesar for
virtuous reasons. And Shakespeare has turned that sentiment into unforgettable poetry.

> This was the noblest Roman of them all:
> All the conspirators, save only he,
> Did that they did in envy of great Caesar;
> He, only in a general honest thought
> And common good to all, made one of them.
> His life was gentle, and the elements
> So mix'd in him that Nature might stand up
> And say to all the world, "This was a man!"
>
> (5.5.68-75)

The words "of them all" in the first line refer to the assassins. But as
these lines develop, they also mean the noblest Roman of all past history.
This was the Roman paragon of a man. And there is a deep poignancy
in Antony's pronouncing these words over the self-slain Brutus, however
dutifully or formally. For within a few years Antony, too, would fall on
his sword before the power of Caesar.

To people who remembered and cherished republican ideals Brutus was
the last and noblest of the old Romans. In Renaissance Florence his reputation took a sudden lift from the curse Dante had put on it. Dante came
to be understood as having written allegorically, punishing Brutus and
Cassius for their crime against idealized world government, not for their
deeds against an actual tyrant. Later Dante was judged to have been simply
mistaken.[4] By the early eighteenth century Brutus was widely accepted
as a hero needing no apologies. Swift has a worldly-wise Gulliver meet
with him as the most worthy shade to be found in the underworld.

The Governor at my request gave the sign for Caesar and Brutus to
advance towards us. I was struck with a profound veneration at the
sight of Brutus, and could easily discover the most consummate virtue,
the greatest intrepidity and firmness of mind, the truest love of his
country and general benevolence for mankind in every lineament of

his countenance. I observed with much pleasure that these two persons were in good intelligence with each other, and Caesar freely confessed to me, that the greatest actions of his own life were not equal by many degrees to the glory of taking it away. I had the honour to have much conversation with Brutus; and was told, that his ancestor Junius, Socrates, and Epaminondas [the self-sacrificing Theban general], Cato the younger, Sir Thomas More and himself were perpetually together: a *sextumvirate* to which all the ages of the world cannot add a seventh.[5]

Brutus as the most heartless or senseless of murderers and Brutus as the peerless scourge of a tyrant: these two interpretations cannot be reconciled. Yet both continue to fascinate students of the past and to exercise the moral judgments of scholars. In large measure, however, modern history has reduced both Caesar and Brutus to smaller dimensions in the centuries of Roman politics.

Ronald Syme, for example, seems to have deliberately avoided recounting the scene of Caesar's death in his influential book, *The Roman Revolution*. He attempts instead to trace the interconnections of hundreds of events in the moral, economic, social, political, and military life of Rome. He places Brutus and Cassius among dozens of powerful senators who brought Caesar down for a variety of motives, mainly venal. These were the privileged oligarchs of the late republic, who spoke in high terms about liberty and constitutional order but were in fact as willing as Caesar was to alter the rules for personal advantage. "They stood," Syme writes, "not merely for the traditions and institutions of the Free State, but very precisely for the dignity and interests of their own order. Liberty and the laws are high-sounding words. They will often be rendered, on a cool estimate, as privilege and vested interests."[6] In the large picture the conspirators were all caught in a bewildering social upheaval. Over the course of centuries Rome had acquired control over vast territories far from Italy. The political institutions of a free city-state were not adequate for governing such an empire; they gave way to grasping power struggles between military conquerors, with their subordinates and clients, on the one hand, and the heirs of the old aristocracy, on the other. The result was bloodshed through many generations. Caesar and Brutus were successive victims in a chain of murders and suicides linking all the great leaders from Sulla to Pompey to Cato to Cicero to Antony and Cleopatra.

This third, geopolitical interpretation treats the dictatorship and death of Julius Caesar as a sketchy prologue to the forty-year reign of Caesar

Augustus. The final result was world peace at the cost of liberty. But the alternative had been unending, demoralizing civil war—an alternative palpable and intolerable to the Romans who at last celebrated the beginnings of perpetual empire.

In one aspect, then, Brutus and Cassius were but children of their time: helplessly tainted late republicans, moving warily through the streets with sharp daggers under their togas for self-defense. In another aspect they were inept patriots. They could not effect a coup d'état; they could not secure the backing even of the senate, which promptly ratified all the acts of the murdered Caesar; they could not even save themselves from the tumult of an anarchic city or the consolidation of new imperial forces. But in this third aspect they were liberators indeed, unwitting instruments of a revolution larger than their own plans. In killing Caesar they eliminated a sick and aging dictator. Perhaps they cut him off from a foolhardy eastern expedition. They thus opened the way for the rise of his younger, stronger, more complex and powerful successor.

A fourth interpretation of the assassination might be called theological. This is the view that the gods intervened in the death of Caesar and its consequences in history. Christian tradition places the Roman civil wars as vain strivings just before the birth of the Prince of Peace during the Pax Romana of Augustus. Or there is the ecclesiastical miracle that the Roman Empire prepared a means for the rapid spread of the gospel throughout the civilized world. But within ancient Rome other potent divinities claimed their own influence. These are the forces behind the prophecies, omens, and wonders that surrounded the Ides of March. Ancient historians record what Shakespeare would make famous: earthquakes, monsters and the resurrected dead in the streets, comets in the sky, blood in the rain, soothsayers and auguries of disaster, the ghost that visited Brutus at Philippi. These may seem mere superstitions or elaborations worked up after the fact, to heighten the great man's fall. But they also point to a persisting enigma about Caesar, his conviction of his own divinity.

Divus Julius is the title of Suetonius's writings about Caesar. It has been borrowed for Stefan Weinstock's study of how Caesar conceived and attempted to establish a ruler cult within the public religion of Rome. To a cynical eye this might seem the ultimate manipulation of am imperial dictator—to enjoin worship as well as obedience from his subjects. Weinstock, however, argues that Caesar was "an imaginative and daring religious reformer . . . a reformer, moreover, who did not want to appear as an innovator, nor to spread a new philosophy of life, but to be guided by tradition; and yet one who in the end radically broke with it."[7] He summarizes the necessities of empire which pushed Caesar to this radical break:

It was probably on his Eastern campaigns that Caesar conceived the plan of a Roman version of the ruler cult. There it was a political and religious necessity to claim for himself what had been due to the kings of the East; Dea Roma as a religious bond no longer sufficed to hold the parts of his empire together. In Rome itself his new position was to be prepared in the Roman fashion by the honours mentioned above. [These were honors that outnumbered those of any predecessor, but that had been granted to earlier figures like Romulus, Lucius Junius Brutus, and Cicero.] In the past the gods had represented a continuity, a never-changing authority, in contrast to that of the annual magistrates. Now their authority was to be shared by Caesar, who therefore required religious backing.

In other words, Caesar was conscientiously taking new powers upon himself for the greater glory of Rome. But the trappings of full divinity derived from eastern customs; the preparations for a cult were about to be realized just as the assassins made their move; and it is an open question how deeply Caesar the world conqueror had been influenced in the East to think of himself as divine.

These preparations were intensified when the Parthian campaign became imminent. In Parthia Caesar meant to appear as a legitimate king, the heir to all its political and religious traditions, and he wished to be honoured accordingly. It may well be that he drove into Rome in his triumph of 46 in a chariot with white horses precisely because that was how the Persian kings used to appear. Later he wore, or planned to wear, the Eastern tunic and wanted to wear the diadem. In Rome his house received a pediment; he wore the shoes of the Alban kings and rode like a king into Rome on horseback. His cult was decreed and a priesthood created. During his long absence his cult was to become established in Rome and Italy and perhaps to prepare for more. The Parthian victory would have consolidated his empire in the East, and the West would have followed suit.

(Weinstock, p. 413)

The assassination was therefore momentous in more than politics. Brutus and Cassius may have understood that they were cutting a would-be god down to limp flesh and congealing blood. And yet as events turned out they were caught in an enormous cosmic irony. Within a year, on January 1,

43, Caesar was consecrated by the senate; his divine name, Divus Iulius, was confirmed in 42. He was established as a god. He had a cult with a priest and a temple in Rome; the latter was built in the Forum, where Caesar's body had been cremated by the mob of rioters, and it remained there in the midst of public life for centuries. Coins were circulated bearing Caesar's image as a god, so that Jesus' remark about rendering unto Caesar what was Caesar's literally meant rendering unto a god what was a god's. Later emperors, beginning with Augustus, also followed the practice of becoming gods. The process by which they were confirmed reflects back on the events of the assassination. The senate debated their worthiness, in a kind of trial or Judgment of the Dead. "Considering the case of Caesar," Weinstock remarks, "one soon realizes that such a Judgment of the Dead was held at the meeting of the Senate on 17 March 44" (pp. 388-89).

The speeches of Brutus and Mark Antony over Caesar's body recapitulate this judgment of Caesar's divinity. The conspirators urged that Caesar was a tyrant unworthy of a funeral. Mark Antony, whom Caesar had already named as the *flamen* or priest of his cult, successfully argued for a funeral at public expense and conducted the funeral on March 20 with rituals of oratory, display, and divine honors that must have been carefully outlined by Caesar himself (Weinstock, p. 354).

In short, the murderers of Caesar became in time his hapless accomplices, exalting him suddenly and dramatically from worldiy power to a place among the enduring gods.

However it was interpreted, the assassination of Caesar remained a dramatic memory. Whether it was a sensational murder, a unique act of tyrannicide, a pivotal moment of revolution, or a transformation of a man into a god, it was a scene to arrest and fascinate great numbers of people both immediately and long afterward.

There are evident reasons why this had to be so. The conspirators' express aim was to bring down the greatest man of their time for just cause. And Caesar was himself a consummate master of public impressions. What he wore, how he moved or was carried, whether he stood or sat, how he was placed in relation to others around him, all mattered and were noticed in the frequent ceremonies and political gatherings of Rome. This was public life without newspapers or other intermediaries between a hierarchy of leaders and a large public of citizens who watched their daily appearances and felt their effects. Any unofficial appeal to a public, such as circulating a notice or calling a rally, might easily be suppressed by authority. The assassins had to both strike and plainly justify their deed in the same public gesture. Accordingly, they surrounded Caesar in a public place. They acted under color of their office, as senators rising against him in the senate. They each took a stab, to show both their solidarity and their numerous individual judgments against him. As it happened, the senate meeting that day was in a building built by Pompey, in a chamber with Pompey's statue. They killed Caesar at its base, as if to undo his conquest over that predecessor. And they left the body as it fell, to signify its unworthiness for further regard. That this was not enough was soon proved by events. But this was action without words, calculated to leave a powerful impression and get an attentive hearing for later words of justification. And it was action that was overcome only by other action, by the ritual and display of a calculated funeral.

The full drama of the event can therefore hardly be suggested by any single historical account. But fortunately for us and for Shakespeare, there was a source from antiquity which managed to give full play both to Caesar and to Brutus, and to the long sweep of history and law and fate in which their lives had meaning. This was the collection of parallel lives written by Plutarch of Chaeronea, a source that gave special color and dignity to the career of Brutus.

Shakespeare drew heavily on Sir Thomas North's English version of Plutarch in writing *Julius Caesar*, and his borrowings, paraphrases, and transformations have been thoroughly scrutinized over the years. To appreciate how closely Shakespeare relied on Plutarch, a reader must consult a work that puts both texts immediately adjacent to each other, like T. J. B. Spencer's edition of Plutarch, quoted above, or a fully annotated edition of the play. The recent Oxford Shakespeare edition also contains a valuable "consecutive discussion" of how the playwright drew upon this source in scene after scene.[8] What such apparatus shows in general is that Shakespeare did not blush to borrow heavily; in many places he observes fine details from Plutarch and includes them, even though a casual observer of the play might barely notice. It seems that he expected many in his audience to have read Plutarch — and indeed North's version was a popular book, running through many editions in Shakespeare's time. Perhaps he felt bound to provide such touches, just as modern plays and films are obliged to satisfy viewers who have already read the book. Some of Shakespeare's scenes do not make complete sense without a familiar knowledge of Roman ways.[9]

But reading Plutarch and Shakespeare side by side creates its own distortions, especially where passages from one are printed as footnotes to the other. Plutarch provides more than colorful details or necessary explanations about Brutus and Caesar. He also places their lives in an inviting pattern of historical writing and views them with his own ample, distanced, well-balanced judgments. His *Lives* deserve to be read for themselves, as many in Shakespeare's audience are sure to have read them. A reader should afford the leisure to take in each long story and see its place in Plutarch's ambitious compendium of anecdotal biographies.

Plutarch grew up in Greece, studied in Athens, and lived most of his life in a remote Greek city. Many incidental remarks in his works show that he cherished the memory of ancient Greece, its Platonic philosophy and its political freedom. But his city, Chaeronea, was the site of Alexander's decisive conquest of the Greek city-states. And Plutarch was born in the reign of Augustus's successor Claudian, long after the Roman Empire was solidly established — though he records stories from older relatives about the battle of Philippi and the Egyptian feasts of Antony and Cleopatra. Plutarch had friends in Rome, visited there, and held Roman citizenship. Perforce he had to feel two deep layers of tradition embedded in the world he knew. As a Roman in the age of Hadrian, he had to acknowledge that ancient Greece was a memory. But as a scholar still writing Greek in Chaeronea, he could also view the most illustrious Romans as successors to older heroes.

The title of North's translation reads, *The Lives of the noble Grecians and Romans, compared together by that grave learned Philosopher and Historiographer, Plutarch of Chaeronea.* Most of Plutarch's career was given to writing moral and philosophical works, dozens of them, later collected as his *Moralia.* It was late in life that he undertook his series of biographies. And so he brought to it a mind seasoned with age; stored with learning and odd information; and practiced in both research and meditation on human nature, history, and the fortunes of the great. He wrote the lives, he said, to provide moral instruction, to excite emulation for noble actions. "Virtue," he wrote in the *Life of Pericles,* "instantly produces by her actions a frame of mind in which the deed is admired and the doer rivalled at one and the same moment. . . . Nobility exercises an active attraction and immediately creates an active impulse, not merely forming an eye-witness's personality by imitation, but producing a settled moral choice from the simple historical knowledge of the action. This is why I have made up my mind to spend my time writing biographies."[10]

In order to set virtue vividly before his readers Plutarch developed two important strategies. One was to select telling little details as well as narratives of famous doings. "For the noblest deeds do not always show men's virtues and vices," he wrote in the *Life of Alexander*, "but oftentimes a light occasion, a word, or some sport, makes men's natural dispositions and manners appear more plain than the famous battles won wherein are slain ten thousand men, or the great armies, or cities won by siege or assault" (Spencer, pp. 7-8). Plutarch's second major strategy was to assemble a large collection of eminent lives and present them in pairs, matching the careers of the greatest Greeks with those of the greatest Romans. To most of these pairs he appended a brief summary comparison, highlighting the most salient strengths of character. This large framework of the *Lives* may seem ingenious, or it may seem awkward and downright pedantic — a colossal monument to the compare-and-contrast assignment that plagued students even in ancient schools. But Plutarch's parallel structure is a crucial feature of the *Life of Brutus*. It makes Brutus stand out as a special kind of Roman.

Altogether Plutarch wrote well over fifty lives; twenty-three pairs and a few single biographies survived and were available to Shakespeare in English. Among the ancient Romans, Brutus's *Life* takes its place with those of Pompey, Cato, Cicero, Caesar, and Mark Antony. Each *Life* has an integrity of its own and repeats some events in a different light. In composing *Julius Caesar*, Shakespeare drew material from the accounts of Caesar and Antony and so fleshed out the finer qualities of Brutus's adversaries, just as Plutarch had done long before. Furthermore, each of these Roman figures is matched with a noble Greek, to bring out a well-defined pattern. Caesar is paired with Alexander, another brilliant world conqueror. Antony is compared to Demetrius, another general with vices as enormous as his virtues. The counterpart to Brutus is Dion, the disciple of Plato who overthrew the Syracusan tyrant Dionysius.

Plutarch introduces Brutus and Dion as men who embodied Platonic philosophy and set it to work in the world.

Methinks that neither the Grecians nor Romans have cause to complain of the Academy, sith they be both alike praised of the same in this present book, in the which are contained the lives of Dion and Brutus. Of the which, the one of them having been very familiar with Plato himself, and the other from his childhood brought up in Plato's doctrine, they both (as it were) came out of one self schoolhouse, to attempt the greatest enterprises amongst men. And it is no marvel if they two were much like in many of their doings, proving that true which their schoolmaster Plato wrote of virtue — that to do any noble act in the government of the commonwealth which should be famous and of credit, authority and good fortune must both meet in one self person, joined with justice and wisdom.[11]

Of course many of Plutarch's other heroes were philosophical, too. Cato was a Stoic who died for his principles. Caesar was a renowned intellectual. Alexander was the pupil and patron of Aristotle. Cicero and Demosthenes won victories by their oratory. But Dion and Brutus are here paired as unique: high-minded men who stood out among coarser allies in perilous times. These accounts show philosophy in action in the harsh and dangerous work of confronting tyrants.

Dion had close family ties to Dionysius the Younger. He persuaded that tyrant to study philosophy and even to bring Plato to teach him in Syracuse. But among Dionysius's courtiers Dion was roundly hated. "The chiefest cause of all why they did malice and hate him," Plutarch explains, "was his strange manner of life, that he would neither keep company with them, nor live after their manner." His studious ways made him such an outsider that "Plato himself sometime wrote to him . . . that he should beware of obstinacy, the companion of solitariness, that bringeth a man in the end to be forsaken of everyone" (Baughman, 2: 1781-83).

Brutus was not so badly isolated by philosophy. The corresponding description of this character is one of Plutarch's vivid anecdotes. It shows a man almost comically tolerated as a scholar among soldiers, in this case Pompey's forces when Brutus came among them "to be partaker of the danger" of Caesar's pursuit.

> It is reported that Pompey, being glad and wondering at his coming, when he saw him come to him he rose out of his chair and went and embraced him before them all, and used him as honourably as he could have done the noblest man that took his part. Brutus, being in Pompey's camp, did nothing but study all day long, except he were with Pompey, and not only the days before, but the self same day also before the great battle was fought in the fields of Pharsalia, where Pompey was overthrown. It was in the midst of summer, and the sun was very hot, besides that the camp was lodged near unto marshes; and they that carried his tent tarried long before they came, whereupon, being very weary with travel, scant any meat came into his mouth at dinner-time. Furthermore, when others slept, or thought what would happen the morrow after, he fell to his book, and wrote all day long till night, writing a breviary of Polybius.
>
> (Spencer, p. 105)

Here is the site of battle. The sun is hot. The air is miasmal. Brutus
is underfed and weary from travel. Caesar's approach has everyone tensed
for danger. But while others catch sleep while they can, here is Brutus
wide awake making an abstract of universal history! Plutarch repeats this
image to describe Brutus's habits when he and Cassius were preparing to
face their last battle. Others turned to their rest, but Brutus went back to
his studies. "After he had slumbered a little after supper, he spent all the
rest of the night in dispatching of his weightiest causes; and after he had
taken order for them, if he had any leisure left him, he would read some
book till the third watch of the night; at what time the captains, petty-
captains, and colonels did use to come to him" (Spencer, p. 148).

Plutarch heightens this impression by making Cassius a harsh foil to
the gentler Brutus. As we saw earlier, he claims that Brutus was drawn
into Cassius's murderous conspiracy. Later he shows Brutus behaving kindly
toward a difficult ally.

> Men reputed [Cassius] commonly to be very skilful in wars, but
> otherwise marvellous choleric and cruel, who sought to rule men by
> fear rather than with lenity; and on the other side he was too familiar
> with his friends and would jest too broadly with them. But Brutus
> in contrary manner, for his virtue and valiantness was well-beloved
> of the people and his own, esteemed of noblemen, and hated of no
> man, not so much as of his enemies; because he was a marvellous
> lowly and gentle person, noble minded, and would never be in any
> rage, nor carried away with pleasure and covetousness; but had ever
> an upright mind with him, and would never yield to any wrong or
> injustice, the which was the chiefest cause of his fame, of his rising,
> and of the good will that every man bare him; for they were all
> persuaded that his intent was good.
>
> (Spencer, p. 139)

Yet these accounts do not imply that Dion and Brutus were fastidious,
well-meaning pedants who had no business being in court or camp among
treacherous men. Quite the contrary. Plutarch presents them as strong,
daring, capable leaders. That is what makes them fascinating. They could
devote themselves to philosophy and still be effective in politics. They
came close to being the ideal Platonists, statesmen who could discipline
their minds and prevail in trials of power.

In Plutarch's judgment, it was only very narrowly that Brutus failed.
Until the last moments at Philippi he had victory within his grasp. If he
had known of a naval victory over the fleets carrying his opponents'

supplies, he might well have planned his battles differently. He might have defeated Octavian and Antony so sharply that no emperor ever came to be. In the course of this biography, Plutarch sees into all the major versions of Brutus's significance. He allows that he could be ruthless. He notes that civil wars could be worse than the rule of a dictator. He stresses Brutus's courage against tyranny. Yet in the end he joins a geopolitical and a theological view in one momentous sentence. "Howbeit the state of Rome (in my opinion) being now brought to that pass that it could no more abide to be governed by many lords but required one only absolute governor, God, to prevent Brutus that it should not come to his government, kept this victory from his knowledge, though indeed it came but a little too late" (Spencer, p. 165). And the gods underscored this point by sending Caesar's ghost to Brutus on the eve of battle.

One further impression from Plutarch deserves to be mentioned for its effect on Shakespeare and the modern world. When the playwright took up North's translation he had to turn the pages of a large and heavy volume. The fifty lives in the 1579 edition run to over 1,100 pages in one great folio, a ponderous printed monument of the ancient world. It might seem that Plutarch included every worthy of Greece and Rome down to the establishment of the empire. And in the traditional order of the lives Dion and Brutus came last among those that are paired, Brutus last of all. Plutarch indicates elsewhere that these lives were not the last to be written. But they were traditionally given the final place, so that Brutus followed Pompey, Caesar, Cicero, and Antony. Whether calculated or not, this arrangement gives Brutus the last word on republican Rome. The bookworm in the armed camp greets the bookworm who takes up Plutarch in the library, with the reassurance that the bullies of this world are not the only enduring heroes. Shakespeare followed Plutarch's lead to create two magnificent dangerous bookworms in *Julius Caesar* and *Hamlet*.

Figure 1. The assassination scene in Shakespeare's *Julius Caesar*, from Edwin Booth's production at Booth's Theatre in 1871. Watercolor design by Charles Witham, reprinted by permission of the Theatre and Music Collection, Museum of the City of New York. Witham designed this set by imitating Jean-Louis Gérôme's painting *La Mort de César*, to re-create Rome's grandeur on Booth's vast stage. Witham also designed the impressive sets for the 1870 *Hamlet* at Booth's Theatre.

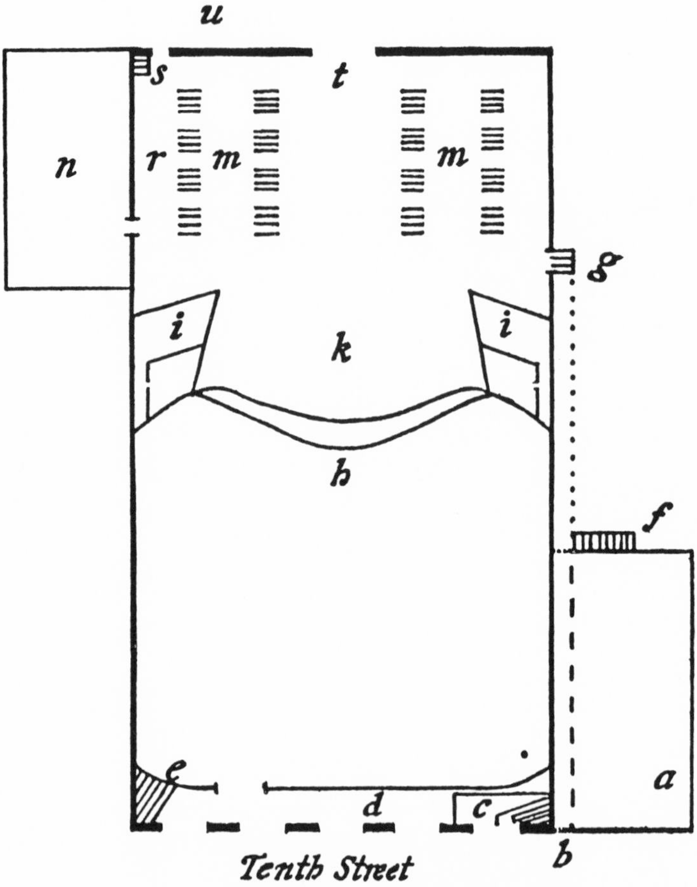

GROUND PLAN OF FORD'S

(After a sketch in the John T. Ford Papers)

a. Building adjoining theater on south (Taltavull's)—*b.* Entrance to corridor, leading to footway and thus up steps to stage door,*g*—*f.* Outside stairs—*c.* Office, and stairs to family circle—*d.* Lobby—*e.* Stairway to dress circle—*h.* Musicians—*k.* Stage—*ii.* First-tier boxes—*mm.* Scenes—*n.* Building adjoining theater on north (dressing rooms, greenroom)—*r.* Passageway—*s.* Rear door (stairs at left, leading below stage) —*t.* Large door (for bringing in scenery, etc.)—*u.* Public alley.

Figure 2a. Ground plan of Ford's Theatre. From George S. Bryan, *The Great American Myth* (New York: Carrick & Evans, 1940).

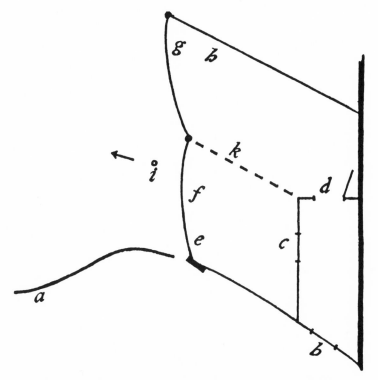

THE "STATE BOX" AT THE TIME OF THE MURDER

a. Apron of stage—*b.* Door into vestibule from dress circle—*c.* Door of nearer box (this remained closed)—*d.* Door of farther box (this remained open—*e.* Lincoln—*f.* Mrs. Lincoln—*g.* Miss Harris—*h.* Major Rathbone—*i.* Spot where Booth landed on stage, near first-tier boxes—*k.* Line of removed partition.

Figure 2b. The "State Box" at the time of the murder. From Bryan, *The Great American Myth.*

Figure 3. Seal of the State of Virginia, as it appeared in the masthead of the Richmond *Whig* in the 1860s. Courtesy of the American Antiquarian Society.

Figure 4. John Wilkes Booth onstage at Ford's Theatre just after the assassination. From *Frank Leslie's Illustrated Newspaper*, May 20, 1865. Courtesy of the American Antiquarian Society. The actor Harry Hawk still stands on stage, Booth has leapt from the upper boxes to our right, and J. B. Stewart is climbing onto the stage to pursue him.

Figure 5. Edwin Booth as Hamlet in 1870. Photograph by Napoleon Sarony. Courtesy of the Hampden-Booth Theatre Library at The Players, New York City.

3

Shakespeare's Tragic Tyrannicides

*T*O FIND a beginning generaliza-
tion about Shakespeare, one can hardly do better than turn to Samuel
Johnson's famous Preface to Shakespeare's *Works* (1765), where he frankly
and sternly takes the poet to task for his incurable love of puns. Johnson
says that Shakespeare's love of punning (or "quibbling") constantly inter-
rupts the development of the strongest or most delicate feelings. Here is
Johnson's judgment in its full sententious gravity:

> What he does best, he soon ceases to do. He is not long soft and
> pathetick without some idle conceit or contemptible equivocation.
> He no sooner begins to move than he counteracts himself; and terror
> and pity, as they are rising in the mind, are checked and blasted by
> sudden frigidity.
>
> A quibble is to Shakespeare what luminous vapours are to the
> traveller; he follows it at all adventures, it is sure to lead him out of
> his way, and sure to engulf him in the mire. It has some malignant
> power over his mind, and its fascinations are irresistible. Whatever
> be the dignity or profundity of his disquisition, whether he be en-
> larging knowledge or exalting affection, whether he be amusing at-
> tention with incidents, or enchaining it in suspense, let but a quibble
> spring up before him, and he leaves his work unfinished. A quibble

31

is the golden apple for which he will always turn aside from his
career, or stoop from his elevation. A quibble, poor and barren as it
is, gave him such delight that he was content to purchase it by the
sacrifice of reason, propriety and truth. A quibble, was to him the
fatal Cleopatra for which he lost the world, and was content to lose
it.[1]

Earlier in the Preface, Johnson claims Shakespeare is the greatest of all
poets because he most accurately represents the world as it is and remains
through all time. "Shakespeare is, above all writers, at least above all
modern writers, the poet of nature; the poet that holds up to his readers
a faithful mirror of manners and of life" (p. 62). But like many other
readers and viewers Johnson yearns to take a long look into a steady mirror.
As he says just a few lines earlier, "The mind can only repose on the
stability of truth." Puns make that impossible. They not only get in the
way or distract from an intensity of feeling; they also subvert the clarity
and certainty of language. They shake the mirror if they do not shatter
it. Near the above passage on Shakespeare's quibbles, Johnson remarks that
for all his excellencies Shakespeare has faults, and they are "faults sufficient
to obscure and overwhelm any other merit." And he states that Shakespeare's admirers "have most reason to complain" precisely here, when
he leads them to moments of intensity, then runs off to toy with equivocal
words (pp. 71, 74).

Johnson's praise and complaint make a good starting point for any reader
baffled by the sheer mass of what we call Shakespeare: the bulky collection
of plays, the libraries of commentary, the warehouses of documents of
theatrical history, the constant docketing of yet more new productions,
more new studies, more new controversies. What is at the heart of it all?
On the one hand, a yearning like Johnson's for a vision of deep and lasting
truth; on the other, a constant, irrepressible urge to indulge in equivocal
play.

To critics like Johnson at his most severe, Shakespeare will be forever
unsatisfying if not daunting. Many readers simply give up hope once they
have struggled through the usual demands of school-prescribed reading.
Elizabethan language is hard to work through in the first place, and then
it turns out to be of uncertain meaning even in the most crucial scenes.
But to readers who can stretch their patience further, Shakespeare yields
an incomparable reward. His puns are a verbal symptom of an inexhaust-
ibly curious mind. And his plays bring together a wealth of characters,
all of whom see the world differently and give voice to human longings

that cannot be reconciled. Shakespeare never yields a single moral vision. He yields a multitude. He holds together many simultaneous ways of viewing the same events, often compressing them with fine control into the explosive power of a single word.

Shakespeare's wordplay was surely fostered by the practical demands of his work in the theater. He wrote for a company that put on repeated performances of the same plays. The layered possibilities of his language therefore could unfold to enrich their meaning and pleasure for an audience that kept returning. This audience was also attuned to complex poetry in the theater and elsewhere, the poetry of Donne and Spenser and the plays in verse of Marlowe and Jonson and many others. And like any good dramatist Shakespeare had to develop a keen sense of the tension that follows every speech. What it seems to mean to the speaker may not be what the next speaker evidently hears, or what the bystander takes in about what it implies. From moment to moment the players hang on each other's words. Every word may count. With a pun, a word counts sharply.

The earliest scenes in *Hamlet* and *Julius Caesar* show just how alert Shakespeare is to stirring possibilities in ambiguous words. When Hamlet first appears, at Claudius's first court, his speeches all pick up and overthrow what seem the formal but well-meaning gestures of the King and Queen:

King.	But now, my cousin Hamlet, and my son —
Hamlet.	A little more than kin, and less than kind.
King.	How is it that the clouds still hang on you?
Hamlet.	No so, my lord, I am too much in the sun.
Queen.	Good Hamlet, cast thy nighted color off,
	And let thine eye look like a friend on Denmark.
	Do not for ever with thy vailed lids
	Seek for thy noble father in the dust.
	Thou know'st 'tis common, all that lives must die,
	Passing through nature to eternity.
Hamlet.	Ay, madam, it is common.
Queen.	If it be,
	Why seems it so particular with thee?
Hamlet.	Seems, madam? nay, it is, I know not "seems."

$$(1.2.64\text{-}76)^2$$

"Son/sun," "common," "seems" all offer Hamlet a chance to talk back petulantly. They make him a conspicuous malcontent in a court that has just come together to ratify Claudius's reign and marriage. He gives the first impression of being a very unpleasant young man, retorting so sarcastically to royal favor and parental reassurance. But as the scene develops we learn that these short answers are outbursts of grief from a mourner who is officially obliged to keep silent about a recent death and an incestuous marriage. As the play develops, we see that Hamlet's life's work will be to answer this king and queen and reveal truths they would prefer to suppress. And these very terms will echo throughout the drama. Hamlet will have to prove whose "son" he is, demonstrate that he is far from "common" or capable of observing common ways, and thread his way through a labyrinth of falsehood and "seeming." What seem very ordinary expressions turn out to be highly charged. Hamlet is the first in the play to hear that. For much of the play he will dance alone around characters who go on talking, unconscious of their own banality. Shakespeare does not merely fool with a few puns here, but shocks the audience toward habits of sharper hearing.

The first scene of *Julius Caesar* may seem more directly in line with Johnson's complaint about distraction. As the play opens, the tribunes Flavius and Murellus come upon a group of idling Roman workmen. They scold them and ask what they are about, and soon get teasing answers from a cobbler. This cobbler does not appear anywhere but in this scene, and his ambiguous replies sound very much like a stand-up routine borrowed from one of Shakespeare's comedies.

Murellus. You, sir, what trade are you?

Cobbler. Truly, sir, in respect of a fine workman, I am but, as you would say, a cobbler.

Murellus. But what trade art thou? Answer me directly.

Cobbler. A trade, sir, that I hope I may use with a safe conscience, which is indeed, sir, a mender of bad soles.

Flavius. What trade, thou knave? thou naughty knave, what trade?

Cobbler. Nay, I beseech you, sir, be not out with me; yet if you be out sir, I can mend you.

Murellus. What mean'st thou by that? Mend me, thou saucy fellow?

Cobbler. Why, sir, cobble you.

Flavius. Thou art a cobbler, art thou?

Cobbler. Truly, sir, all that I live by is with the awl: I meddle with no tradesman's matters, nor women's matters; but withal I am indeed, sir, a surgeon to old shoes; when they are in great danger, I recover them. As proper men as ever trod upon neat's-leather have gone upon my handiwork.

(1.1.9-26)

Some of the punning here turns on words that had different meanings in Shakespeare's time. "Soles" or "souls," "awl" or "all" are obvious, but "cobbler" could also mean "clumsy workman," "out" could mean "worn out" or "out of temper." This exchange is but a tissue of saucy quips in prose, cued to the repetitive blank verse of the tribunes. These lines also stand out as a rare comic passage, and a rare appearance of low characters, in a play that consists mainly of lofty speeches by noble Romans. But this scene is definitely not out of place. As these exchanges continue we see that the lower orders are not unintelligent in Rome. This cobbler is a sturdy citizen, unafraid of a public officer, not about to be pushed around, proud of his useful work. In the next exchange he becomes the spokesman for the group and reveals that the common people have turned out in support of Caesar.

> *Flavius.*   But wherefore art not in thy shop today?
>   Why dost thou lead these men about the streets?
> *Cobbler.*   Truly, sir, to wear out their shoes, to get myself into more
>   work. But indeed, sir, we make holiday to see Caesar, and
>   to rejoice in his triumph.
>
> (1.1.27-31)

And here the tone shifts. The tribunes now make longer speeches, reminding the people that this triumph is for a victory over the Romans, in fact over the blood of Pompey, whom these same commoners used to celebrate just as eagerly. They speak so well that the people feel ashamed and disperse without another word.

> *Flavius.*   See whe'er their basest metal be not mov'd;
>   They vanish tongue-tied in their guiltiness.
>
> (1.1.61-62)

The cocky little shoemaker is silenced, but by good reasons as well as official force. High public speech begins to reach the ears and hearts of friends, Romans, and countrymen. The long, bloody succession of Pompey, Caesar, and Octavian is firmly announced. And Shakespeare, far from running away with a string of puns, makes them work to a serious end. He cuts off the high spirits of a Roman holiday to prepare for the awesome imperiousness of Caesar.

These two passages also reveal more than Shakespeare's control over laughter or wit. They show him exercising his impulses to combine both play and deep seriousness, and on a large scale as well as a small one. *Hamlet* and *Julius Caesar*, in these scenes, reveal contrasting worlds beset by a similar problem. Rome is a world of broad daylight and effective public speech. Hamlet's Denmark is a dark and oppressive castle, where what is said is but a teasing clue to secret crimes or the loneliest anguish. Yet in both plays the central action is the same, the deliberate murder of a tyrant.

The two plays are bound together by many similarities. *Julius Caesar* was written and first performed around 1599, *Hamlet* around 1601. *Hamlet* contains some direct and pointed references to Caesar and his death. The two plays stand apart from Shakespeare's earlier efforts at tragedy, *Titus Andronicus* and *Romeo and Juliet;* they are also separated by several years from *Othello, King Lear,* and *Macbeth.* But most importantly, both plays concentrate on the same political problem, which is nowhere else developed in quite the same terms. Both Brutus and Hamlet undertake to overthrow an established ruler by violence. Both understand that they are engaged in murdering a tyrant. But both wear out long hours intellectualizing their involvement in the blunt fact of murder. Both work hard to explain, to themselves and others, the precise narrow terms that make their deeds conscientious rather than self-interested. Then both give up their own lives gracefully, as the price of what they have done.

We will take up each of these points in full detail, but the conclusion is immediate and inescapable that these plays have to be understood as a balanced pair. Shakespeare created Hamlet for an audience that already knew Brutus very well. Hamlet's intricate character is far less murky if it is understood as an elaboration of that earlier role. Conversely, the patterns Shakespeare sees in Brutus are sharpened by a reading of *Hamlet.* The later play is the poet's fullest gloss on the problems of tyrannicide.

Before Shakespeare turned to Caesar and Brutus he had spent many years writing history plays about civil wars in England. Following a well-worn historical tradition he outlined more than a century of disasters that followed the forced overthrow of a legitimate king. The fall of Richard II in 1399 was succeeded by the guilt-ridden and precarious reigns of Henry IV, Henry V, and Henry VI, then by the bloodshed of the Wars of the Roses. The curse of Richard's overthrow was cured only by the eventual blending of dynastic lines in the birth of Henry VII, the direct ancestor of Elizabeth I. Shakespeare therefore combined patriotism and popular history for many years while he mastered the resources of the theater. And through his series of eight plays on these subjects he returned again and again to one clear theme: overthrowing an established monarch was a deed of enormous evil. *Julius Caesar* bears many similarities to these history plays, including close reliance on a well-known source. The Roman story in fact enables

Shakespeare to sum up and project his historical work in one grand and distanced production. Brutus kills Caesar, in the greatest overthrow recorded in history, and so lets loose the incalculable suffering of an empire swept by anarchy.

Hamlet takes a long step further in the direction of tragedy because it focuses on the inner life and torment of the hero. *Caesar* is a play of public speeches; Hamlet is a play of soliloquies. In *Caesar* Shakespeare was constrained to represent well-known figures from history: Caesar, Brutus, Cassius, Mark Antony, Octavian. He could not alter their characters very much or completely isolate one of them from the public fame they had shared for centuries. But in *Hamlet* he was free to rewrite the material of an obscure older play. He could turn from the massive dimensions of an ancient empire to the confines of a single castle in a remote kingdom. He could adjust circumstances to make just one character the center of the play.

Shakespeare's decisions to write *Caesar* soon after completing his cycle of histories and *Hamlet* soon after *Caesar* were surely not random. He did not just happen upon Plutarch, or stumble into the *Hamlet* plot. This sequence bespeaks an orderly development, an exploration that was to lead Shakespeare away from history into tragedy (until he emerged into Roman daylight again in *Antony and Cleopatra*). And it was to lead to a most puzzling culmination in the character of Hamlet. For here is not the orthodox Elizabethan version of the killer of a king. Here is an assassin on stage who has long won the audience's sympathy and approval: a scrupulous, conscience-ridden man who at last finds a way to purify a kingdom through regicide. Shakespeare's restless imagination and moral curiosity make this further turn of the screw. What if there were a Brutus who succeeded? What if his act could be confined so that only the guilty suffer, or the inflictions on the innocent immediately wound the man who makes them? What if that man measured himself with honest self-awareness against the most stringent ethical standards and still found the courage to act?

Shakespeare's Brutus embodies a much simpler range of questions. His act against Caesar is foredoomed by the well-known facts of history. The concentrated power Caesar represents is too enormous to be destroyed. And for all his philosophizing Shakespeare's Brutus is too simpleminded to understand his own implication in evil. Early and late he talks himself into being a purely honorable man. He blinds himself to the necessary dirty work of slashing living flesh, manipulating a crowd, or extorting cash for an army. Instead he works up masterful verbal arrangements, hollow but resounding:

> If then that friend demand why Brutus rose against Caesar, this is my answer: Not that I lov'd Caesar less, but that I lov'd Rome more. Had you rather Caesar were living, and die all slaves, than that Caesar were dead, to live all freemen? As Caesar lov'd me, I weep for him; as he was fortunate, I rejoice at it; as he was valiant, I honor him; but, as he was ambitious, I slew him. There is tears for his love; joy for his fortune; honor for his valor; and death for his ambition.
>
> (3.2.21-29)

This is hypnotic nonsense. How can there be feeling in language like this, where weeping leads to rejoicing and then "I slew him" just drops into place? Every sentiment can be matched with its proper cause, sometimes prettily ("honor for his valor"), and Brutus shows no suspicion that anyone might doubt him.

> Who is here so base that would be a bondman? If any, speak, for him have I offended. Who is here so rude that would not be a Roman? If any, speak, for him have I offended. Who is here so vile that will not love his country? If any, speak, for him have I offended. I pause for a reply.
>
> (3.2.29-34)

This speech might be tolerable if Brutus were addressing a mirror and nerving himself for the deed or if he were rallying his followers. But this is Brutus before an angry mob; this is his one chance to explain a shocking murder. He is too innocent to suppose that a cunning man like Mark Antony will mock these words with ruthless innuendo and a display of deep feeling.

Shakespeare never lets up on Brutus's innocence. He first appears as an almost willing prey to temptation. ("Into what dangers would you lead me, Cassius?") He last appears running upon his sword, but only after politely shaking hands all around and congratulating his servant for a life with "some smatch of honor in it." This Brutus has gentle virtues. Like Caesar, he can be remarkably kind. He goes out of his way to comfort servants and subordinates. He hears out Cassius's fulminations and answers them firmly, while suppressing his own private grief. He is the only male character in the play to show anything like respect toward a woman. But his language is everywhere pompous or absentminded, even in soliloquy. On the eve of the murder, just before he meets the other conspirators, he goes over the grounds of complaint against Caesar. He reasons alone. But the speech is extremely abstract, and Brutus himself is numb to what it means.

> Th' abuse of greatness is when it disjoins
> Remorse from power; and to speak truth of Caesar,
> I have not known when his affections sway'd
> More than his reason. But 'tis a common proof
> That lowliness is young ambition's ladder. . . .
>
> (2.1.18-22)

Brutus goes on like this for two dozen lines, rehearsing a string of contingent ideas: general considerations indicate assassination of a tyrant; Caesar may be ambitious, enough to turn tyrant, therefore he should be prevented; objections may be raised; yet they could be fully answered. These quoted lines, however, undercut this whole line of reasoning. What Brutus directly, personally knows about Caesar is that so far he has *not* been swayed by passions like ambition. "I have *not* known when his affections sway'd / More than his reason." Caesar might become ambitious, perhaps, if given more power. But that is a merely speculative possibility. And worse than this gap between abstraction and direct experience is a gap between Brutus and his own frailties. "Th' abuse of greatness is when it disjoins / Remorse from power." Brutus feels no remorse, here or later. He never questions whether he might abuse power himself. It does not occur to him that killing Caesar will involve him in seizing power, or that lowliness could be a guise for his own ambition.

Such men are dangerous. But they cannot be tragic. Brutus never reaches an awareness of having done anything cruel or treacherous, not even when he sees a ghost. Before Philippi he boasts that neither Octavian nor Caesar himself was quite worthy of his sword: "O, if thou wert the noblest of thy strain, / Young man, thou couldst not die more honorable" (5.1.59-60). In the end he is driven to defeat and he turns that honorable sword upon himself—but never that honorable mind. He goes to his death saying merely the proper thing:

> Farewell, good Strato. Caesar, now be still,
> I kill'd not thee with half so good a will.
>
> (5.5.50-51)

Hamlet assigns this kind of moral meandering to Polonius. Claudius can speak in moral contradictions, and Hamlet learns to, but they both

know exactly what they are doing. The conflict between them is so intense
because they are both so quick, strong, and self-aware.

> Though yet of Hamlet our dear brother's death
> The memory be green, and that it us befitted
> To bear our hearts in grief, and our whole kingdom
> To be contracted in one brow of woe,
> Yet so far hath discretion fought with nature
> That we with wisest sorrow think on him
> Together with remembrance of ourselves.
> Therefore our sometime sister, now our queen,
> Th' imperial jointress to this warlike state,
> Have we, as 'twere with a defeated joy,
> With an auspicious, and a dropping eye,
> With mirth in funeral, and with dirge in marriage,
> In equal scale weighing delight and dole,
> Taken to wife; nor have we herein barr'd
> Your better wisdoms, which have freely gone
> With this affair along. For all, our thanks.
>
> (1.2.1-16)

So Claudius addresses his first court with such firm control that he cannot
even be called a hypocrite. Hamlet's quibbling answers, discussed earlier,
are the only hint of protest.

Hamlet faces political impossibilities in challenging such a king. Claudius controls this court. He has married the old king's widow and put
Denmark on war alert against Fortinbras or any other enemy. Even if he
is guilty of murder, he cannot be openly attacked or convincingly accused;
he has forcefully seized the throne, and he holds it vigilantly and strongly.
At the end of this first appearance, Hamlet, left alone, can only cry to
himself about his father's sudden death, followed by his mother's incestuous marriage and the coronation of this "satyr." "But break my heart,
for I must hold my tongue" (1.2.159). Throughout the play Hamlet is
boxed in by a king who remains safely guarded and acts quickly to
anticipate any possible threat.

This political problem is compounded by personal dilemmas. Brutus
was one of a large band of assassins, who could support each other not as
conspirators but as liberators working against Caesar's monarchic conspiracy. Shakespeare also avoids mentioning Brutus's involved family relations
with Caesar, and the play shows Brutus allied with a wife who shares his

lofty ideals. But Hamlet must work alone; at almost every turn he must break off or betray an important bond. He is pitted against his uncle, who is married to his mother. He is confined to Elsinore and spied upon by old friends. The one woman he cares for is obedient to her father, the most thoroughly pompous of courtiers.

And Hamlet's innermost conscience is divided. Brutus can appeal to the republican traditions of Roman citizenship, and act and die by that single measure of human fulfilment. Hamlet is troubled by more complicated codes. Hamlet the Dane seeks justice for a murder and a usurpation that have befouled the kingdom. But he is also personally involved. Hamlet the son is exhorted to avenge his father's murder. Hamlet the heir has been cheated of the crown. Hamlet the scholar, moreover, knows that ghosts can be deceivers. And as a Christian he bears a burden of anxiety for his immortal soul. He recognizes that he was already grief-stricken and perhaps a scholarly melancholiac before he got any report of the ghost's haunting the battlements. He refrains from making a step that might merely destroy himself.

> The spirit that I have seen
> May be a dev'l, and the dev'l hath power
> T' assume a pleasing shape, yea, and perhaps,
> Out of my weakness and my melancholy,
> As he is very potent with such spirits,
> Abuses me to damn me.
>
> (2.2.598-603)

These well-known problems in the play stand out when set against the simpler architecture of Brutus's plot. By themselves they are sufficient to explain Hamlet's delays or paralysis, or even the possibility that he is pushed beyond feigning into real madness. To balance all these considerations is a feat of mind for any actor, any audience, or any critic—leaving aside the well-worn theories that Hamlet is a congenital-Oedipal-climatological-diabolical-medical anomaly.

Our concern in any case is with Hamlet the tyrannicide, and his problems are finally insoluble. Given the closed political regime that Claudius controls, the prince cannot murder the king. He would have to make one of three sacrifices, none of which is tolerable. One is his own life, which would likely be cut off in the attempt, whether or not he succeeds. It cannot be risked until success is certain, for there is no one else to set things right in Denmark. Another is his honor, his long-developed character as a just and noble man. Unless he can prove the king is a usurper, and with more than ghostly testimony, he is bound to be considered an ambitious rival or a crazed malcontent for rising in arms. The third sacrifice is Hamlet's soul. If he kills without just cause and, as is likely, dies in the act, he will suffer eternal horrors worse than those the ghost dares not utter. The famous "To be or not to be" soliloquy makes good sense in light of this danger. It is spoken just before Hamlet stages his play before the king; he can hardly be contemplating lonely suicide when he is just about to spring this hopeful stratagem. But he has long been considering how he "might his quietus make" (or pay off an old debt) with a "bare bodkin" (or naked dagger). This would be in an assassination attempt, at the risk of his own life. And, still not knowing whether the ghost might be the pleasing shape of the devil, Hamlet must ponder the cosmic consequences and regret them.

> Thus conscience does make cowards of us all,
> And thus the native hue of resolution
> Is sicklied o'er with the pale cast of thought,
> And enterprises of great pitch and moment
> With this regard their currents turn awry,
> And lose the name of action.
>
> (3.1.82-87)

Caught in this web of frustrations Hamlet turns to other forms of action. Like Lucius Junius Brutus, the legendary founder of Rome, he feigns madness. That makes him unpredictable and puts the king and court off balance in relating to him. He can say the wildest things because they seem aimless. He can insult and provoke. He can seem by turns dangerous and then harmless. But this device has its costs, too, beginning with his ruthless manipulation of Ophelia.

Hamlet also turns with brilliance to managing the actors who stop at Elsinore. Unlike the senate at Rome, the court under Claudius seems to have no public life. The king decides all matters of importance and keeps his able counselors, ambassadors, and courtiers busily dispersed. But Hamlet's staging of a play serves to bring them together. It holds a mirror up to Claudius, and excites him to betray his own guilt. It thus makes public the ghost's version of old Hamlet's death, so that some alert viewers might have their suspicions aroused.

But this project, too, turns awry. The performance causes Claudius to cry out and break away, confirming Hamlet's trust that the ghost has told him the truth. But afterward come unexpected consequences.

In the first place, no one else seems to understand what has happened. Claudius, Hamlet, and Horatio have seen why the play was suddenly stopped. But everyone else is either too dense or too loyal to the king to suppose he could be upset over his own crime. He deftly explains his outrage as the result of Hamlet's antic misbehavior: his setting the players up to show a regicide, perhaps, or his shouting out commentaries insulting Gertrude's marriage. Whatever his swift excuse, Claudius turns his court back to blaming Hamlet. Rosencrantz and Guildenstern, Polonius, and Gertrude all charge him with offending the king. So much for the one opportunity to publish Claudius's crimes.

Next, Hamlet comes upon Claudius unguarded just moments after he has revealed his certain guilt. But the king appears on his knees in an attempt at prayer. At this point in *Caesar* an actual murder occurred, followed by a theatrical exposition of its meaning, in the debates between Brutus and Mark Antony. Here the theatrical indictment for a murder occurs, followed by this scene where Hamlet at last draws his sword, then puts it up again. Just as Antony's funeral oration forces the audience to see Caesar anew as a leader badly wronged, so this scene sets Claudius forth not as the crafty villain he has been but as another complex conscience. Hamlet has forced him not to death, a merely political solution to his crime, but repentance instead. However briefly, Claudius makes a claim on our sympathies as he struggles with cosmic questioning not much different from Hamlet's own.

> My fault is past, but, O, what form of prayer
> Can serve my turn? "Forgive me my foul murther"?
> That cannot be, since I am still possess'd
> Of those effects for which I did the murther:
> My crown, mine own ambition, and my queen.
> May one be pardon'd and retain th' offense?
> In the corrupted currents of this world
> Offense's gilded hand may shove by justice,
> And oft 'tis seen the wicked prize itself
> Buys out the law, but 'tis not so above:
> There is no shuffling, there the action lies
> In his true nature, and we ourselves compell'd
> Even to the teeth and forehead of our faults,
> To give in evidence. What then? What rests?

Try what repentance can. What can it not?
Yet what can it, when one can not repent?

(3.3.51-66)

The anguished plea that follows shows him caught in a perfect trap, calling for help while resolving to strive on somehow by himself. The words might well have come from Hamlet's lips.

O wretched state! O bosom black as death!
O limed soul, that struggling to be free
Art more engag'd! Help, angels! Make assay,
Bow, stubborn knees, and heart, with strings of steel,
Be soft as sinews of the new-born babe!
All may be well.

(3.3.67-72)

So Claudius falls to his knees, just as Hamlet appears. Obviously, there can be no satisfactory assassination at this point. Hamlet makes the notorious excuse that he must wait to be sure of sending Claudius's soul to hell. As the king rises with a sigh from his useless prayer, Hamlet moves on to sink verbal daggers in his mother's ears, which bring her to repentance, too.

Repentance for sin thus undermines the quest with which Hamlet began, to prove and punish usurpation of the kingdom. The result of holding a mirror up to the court is that it has no good effect on the other courtiers, and for a moment it is all too effective on the soul of the guilty king.

Hamlet's final effort short of regicide is to attack the king's satellites, Gertrude and Polonius. The first he handles so roughly she calls out for help. The second, hidden behind the arras, answers her cries and is immediately stabbed and slain. But as a result of this violence Hamlet's original strategies are completely dashed. Murdering Polonius is the last blow that drives the innocent Ophelia to genuine madness and death. It brings Laertes home, bloodthirsty to avenge *his* father's murder. And it supplies Claudius with the perfect pretext for sending Hamlet out of the kingdom to be put to death.

By the end of Act 3, all Hamlet's plans and efforts to undo a tyranny have been checked and defeated. He is closely guarded and doomed to execution. His name is besmirched as a madman and a murderer. Claudius is, if anything, more secure on his throne.

Hamlet's escape and return to Denmark lead to a completely different situation. His actions now turn on a new set of motives and principles. Once he discovers that the king directly plotted to kill him, his primary motive is no longer justice or even revenge. These are now the ostensible motives for Laertes's plotting to assassinate the prince. Hamlet is now threatened directly. He must act in self defense; in that way, killing Claudius can be justified before even his highest court of conscience. Witness his calm dismissal of Rosencrantz and Guildenstern to execution in his place:

> Why, man, they did make love to this employment,
> They are not near my conscience. Their defeat
> Does by their own insinuation grow.
>
> (5.2.57-59)

What directly follows is his determination to kill the king, his acceptance of murder as a lesser evil than allowing this tyrant further range.

> Does it not, think thee, stand me now upon—
> He that hath kill'd my king and whor'd my mother
> Popp'd in between th' election and my hopes,
> Thrown out his angle for my proper life,
> And with such coz'nage—is't not perfect conscience
> To quit him with this arm? And is't not to be damn'd,
> To let this canker of our nature come
> In further evil?
>
> (5.2.63-70)

The Hamlet who returns in Act 5 is palpably older and more settled than the high-strung young man who anguished through the earlier scenes of the play. The gravediggers make the surprising explicit point that he is now thirty years old; born when the old king was in his prime thirty years ago; a playfellow of Yorick, who has been in his grave twenty-three years. The exact age is not important. But our sense of an older Hamlet is. He has now passed through a shadow of death. He has left behind the ghost and the directive influence of his father. He is ready to stand by himself.

The gravedigging scene makes jokes of what used to be the deepest worries on his mind: suicide, dying in self-defense, the decay and persistence of a body in the grave, punctilious niceties of law and conscience. All are scoffed away in a punning match when Hamlet and Horatio loom up over the graveyard.

Moments later, at the funeral of Ophelia, Hamlet fearlessly jumps into the grave. As he does so he identifies himself in a new way. He is not the prince any longer. "This is I, / Hamlet the Dane!" (5.1.257-58). Though it will never be completely recognized by others, Hamlet now knows himself as the rightful king. The proofs are clear, and Claudius has admitted to heaven that his reign is a usurpation. Hamlet therefore is the direct heir, though he remains, as it were, the king incognito. At last he understands this himself and no longer needs to quail at undoing his kingdom's enemy. In the opening lines of the play, the nervous sentinels call for the password, "Long live the King!" Now that king appears, not as a ghost or a usurper, but in a vigorous adult Hamlet who defies Laertes (the image of his former self) as a puny pretender.

The final scene is a ritual of a royal dying. The queen blunders into drinking poison from the king's chalice, just as she has blundered into the poisonous life of being his consort. Hamlet and Laertes exchange wounds, then exchange forgivenesses. The king is named in open court as the murderer of them all. Hamlet then stabs him with the envenomed blade and forces the poisoned drink down his throat. "Here, thou incestious, murd'rous, damned Dane, / Drink off this potion!" (5.2.325-26). Claudius's own evil is turned into himself by Hamlet's hand and he dies, as the avenger had hoped, with enormous sins on his head. Laertes immediately supplies a comment exculpating Hamlet: "He is justly served, / It is a poison temper'd by himself." Hamlet survives just long enough to prevent Horatio from a Roman death, so that Horatio can preserve and defend Hamlet's fame, even to Fortinbras who will now inherit the crown. When Fortinbras appears, Horatio promises just such an explanation:

> And let me speak to th' yet unknowing world
> How these things came about. So shall you hear
> Of carnal, bloody, and unnatural acts,
> Of accidental judgments, casual slaughters,
> Of deaths put on by cunning and forc'd cause,
> And in this upshot, purposes mistook
> Fall'n on th' inventors' heads.
>
>   (5.2.379-85)

Fortinbras ends the play by singling Hamlet out for a royal military funeral, just as Antony and Octavian had singled Brutus out for honor after death. But Brutus died in despair of defeating Caesar; Hamlet is borne off in triumph. The cannons fire to honor him, now that Claudius has drunk his final rouse.

Hamlet is of course much more complicated than this account suggests.

It plays over many themes besides tyrannicide, themes that could be explored just as deeply as characteristic Shakespearean preoccupations: revenge, madness, the conflict between political realism and princely poeticizing, the thin membrane of imagination that separates the world from the stage, or the commonplaces of familiar life from the mysteries of the universe.

Nevertheless, the idea of a just and successful tyrannicide remains essential to this play. As a straight avenger, Hamlet is a poor second to Laertes. As an overburdened mind, he must yield the palm (or the willow branch) to Ophelia. As a master of crafty maneuver, he keeps even pace with Claudius. His unique appeal is rooted in his steadfastness in a cause, the cause of overthrowing a usurper. Hamlet keeps refining it to meet the demands of a questioning, noble mind. He tries to isolate it from his own baser motives, then learns to accept it as indissoluble from the identity to which he was born. Finally, he commits a ruthless killing, completing both his life and his commission from powers beyond this life. He is tragic because he knowingly sacrifices everything else that he values in order to kill Claudius and thereby purify his corrupted world, to give it at least a glimpse of a restored and legitimate reign.

Shakespeare's two plays thus enlarge and reorganize the ancient, mythic adversity between Caesar and Brutus. *Julius Caesar* revitalizes it with all the complexities that Shakespeare found in Plutarch. It gives Brutus his full due, if not his overdose, of honor. But it also reveals his limitations in contrast to the other lofty Romans who surround him, sully him, and ultimately defeat him. *Hamlet* goes much further, to unfold a more daring possibility. It plays with intense and irrepressible teasing around the story of a successful assassin, one who satisfies even the scruples of a learned Christian conscience. No matter how else the play is seen, this pattern remains at its core. Shakespeare has here devised a situation almost certainly impossible in life: the complete, self-contained destruction of a tyrant, with neither a release of anarchic violence nor the subsequent corruption or denigration of the lone assassin's character. After the death of everyone in the Danish line, the realm is left at peace in the hands of Fortinbras, who seems a fair-minded prince and who has Hamlet's dying voice. And though Hamlet dies too soon to explain his full story, we already thoroughly understand it. Countless performances have engraved *Hamlet* into the memories of audiences around the world, and with it a rare vision of liberation through plotted murder.

4

Brother against Brother

$\mathcal{J}$OHN WILKES BOOTH died young in 1865; he was not yet twenty-seven. He had barely won fame as an actor before the assassination of Lincoln overwhelmed every other detail about his life. He was too young to leave a substantial record of a personal career, but everyone knew he was a Booth, one of a family of noted actors. Everyone could read family traits writ large in his public character. He was a "mad" Booth, the favored son of a notoriously eccentric father. Or he was a theatrical Booth, son and brother of actors who often lived on the road and under the shadow of dissipation. Or he was a backwoods Booth, having grown up on an obscure farm in Maryland where the family survived after the father's death in 1852. Or he was the romantic Booth, youngest and handsomest of the acting brothers, and so the most dangerous as a theatrical idol and ladies' man. The Booth family was to prove an easy mark for sensational journalism about the assassin, a source of ready explanations for his outrageous deed.

These explanations influenced the family itself. Edwin, the most distinguished brother, allowed that Wilkes was indeed "wild-brained," young, histrionic, rustic, and spoiled by women. All these explanations appear in a letter he once composed for an elderly historian, to sum up his knowledge of his brother. This letter has often been quoted and tacitly echoed and must therefore be read in full:

I can give you very little information regarding my brother John. I seldom saw him since his early boyhood in Baltimore. He was a rattle-pated fellow, filled with Quixotic notions. While at the farm in Maryland he would charge on horseback through the woods, "spouting" heroic speeches with a lance in his hand, a relic of the Mexican war, given to father by some soldier who had served under Taylor. We regarded him as a good-hearted, harmless, though wild-brained boy, and used to laugh at his patriotic froth whenever secession was discussed. That he was insane on that one point, no one who knew him well can doubt. When I told him that I had voted for Lincoln's reelection he expressed deep regret, and declared his belief that Lincoln would be made king of America; and this, I believe, drove him beyond the limits of reason. I asked him once why he did not join the Confederate army. To which he replied: "I promised mother I would keep out of the quarrel, if possible, and I am sorry that I said so." Knowing my sentiments, he avoided me, rarely visiting my house, except to see his mother, when political topics were not touched upon, at least in my presence. He was of a gentle, loving disposition, very boyish and full of fun, — his mother's darling, — and his deed and death crushed her spirit. He possessed rare dramatic talent, and would have made a brilliant mark in the theatrical world. This is positively all that I know about him, having left him a mere schoolboy when I went with my father to California in 1852. On my return in '56 we were separated by professional engagements, which kept him mostly in the South, while I was employed in the Eastern and Northern States.

I do not believe any of the wild, romantic stories published in the papers concerning him; but of course he may have been engaged in political matters of which I know nothing. All his theatrical friends speak of him as a poor, crazy boy, and such his family think of him.

I am sorry I can afford you no further light on the subject.[1]

This account obviously tries to separate a crazed boy from a family that has suffered on his account. It was written in July 1881, just days after another assassin had shot President Garfield and stirred up all the old stories of Lincoln's death. Here the older brother acknowledges the worst and tries to deflect what he can. Wilkes was "insane" on the subject of secession and "rattle-pated" anyhow. He was pitiable — "a poor, crazy boy" — to both theatrical people and his own family. There was nothing more to say. In other actions Edwin held to the same determined judgment: John Wilkes was a brother he hardly knew; pitiable, young, and erratic; best quietly forgotten. Edwin never went on stage again in Washington. In public and private he kept a strict silence about his brother. In 1869 he finally was able to get the assassin's body released by the War Department, and the family saw to its burial in a new family plot in Baltimore — in a grave without an individual marker. Later Edwin obtained a trunk of his brother's effects, including many rich costumes and heirlooms; according to a famous story, he fed it all to the flames.[2] In 1890 an actress publicly recalled John Wilkes as a talented actor and a lovable man; Edwin wrote to thank her, acknowledging that this was "the first word of compassion for John Wilkes."[3] Meanwhile Asia Booth Clarke, the actors' sister, had written a memoir of her dead brother and compiled an album of sympathetic clippings and letters about him. These albums were hidden away and forgotten, largely because of Edwin's disapproval, and were not published until 1938.[4]

The family had good reasons for maintaining such a grim attitude. They remained in the public eye. They continued in theatrical careers and still sought widespread approval. But after 1865 they were always at risk. The name Booth was poisoned by what had happened in Ford's Theatre. The press would never forget it. An America that reverenced Lincoln could not forgive it. The brothers and sisters had been arrested, jailed, or spied upon in 1865; they had had threats on their lives; their mail had been read; their mementos had been rifled, confiscated, or destroyed. They had been shunned. They were seared by an experience rougher than grief or shame. And it came up again and again. Little wonder if they acquiesced in the widespread conclusion that their brother had carried all their worst features to the grave. That way lay some relief, some salvageable remnant of dignity and peace.

Perhaps there was some truth in this conclusion, too. Perhaps John Wilkes Booth was afflicted with a family trait of melancholia, or came to grief through an intense complication of family circumstances. Perhaps his motives did include the frustrated ambitions of a coddled, darling, rusticated younger brother in a famous and competitive family. There was evidence enough to wear down even Asia, the sympathetic sister, who had shared the younger brother's growing-up years on the farm.

Asia wavers in her memoir of her brother, protesting on one page, "Wilkes Booth was not insane" (UB, p. 138); relenting on another: "If Wilkes Booth was mad, his mind lost its balance between the fall of Richmond and the terrific end" (p. 148); and recording everywhere his contentious, daring, playful, and wild behavior, which grew more intense with the war years. At last it broke out in tirades against Lincoln that even Asia could not understand. "A desperate turn toward evil had come!

I had listened so patiently to these wild tirades, which were the very fever of his distracted brain and tortured heart, that I was powerless to check or soothe" (p. 125).

But the evidence is so fragmentary and so convenient for explaining a national catastrophe that it deserves a pause for skepticism. Hamlet, we should recall, was also considered mad. Hamlet was young and full of fire. Hamlet lost his beloved father and thereafter remained confined to a lonely outpost. Hamlet's antic behavior was readily explained as a result of either frustrated eroticism or thwarted ambition. Hamlet found an outlet in theatrical extravagance. There remains the possibility that John Wilkes Booth, too, could have been mad in craft. At least he must have developed his own autonomous consciousness, quite apart from family maladies or family pressures. As a shrewd adult in wartime he might well have kept his deepest motives hidden or disguised from even his most intimate kin while he made very deliberate plans in league with others.[5]

We should also pause to consider that Edwin's famous letter about his brother was also an act of artistic purgation. The careers of Edwin and John Wilkes Booth reveal two very different sides of nineteenth-century American theater. They correspond almost exactly with the opposite patterns of culture traced in Lawrence Levine's recent book *Highbrow/Lowbrow*. On the one hand was the tradition of popular theater, of tragedy, comedy, music, farce, opera, and variety acts often jumbled together on the same playbill. This was theater as entertainment, addressed to all strata of society. And its audience often responded with a matching exuberance: with heavy applause, stamping, whistling, hissing, catcalls, and missiles hurled to the stage. To be a tragedian here meant competing as a virtuoso performer. The leading roles were often Shakespearean but they were in traditional scripts, cut and revised to bring out great theatrical effects. On the other hand was an emerging conception of the theater as a temple of high art, designed primarily for the spiritual purification of the well dressed and the well behaved. In the later nineteenth century this was the setting for a single performance on a playbill, often a masterwork "restored" to its author's original script, and played with a new, more refined virtuosity. On the one hand, in other words, was a democratic art form, which celebrated Shakespeare as a vigorous American spirit and made his lines the familiar language of scholar and workman alike; on the other hand was an intimidating, esoteric theater (which still affects our modern taste for "legitimate" art), in which Shakespeare was preserved beyond the reach of ordinary people.

John Wilkes Booth clearly lived and thrived in the older medium. In his years of stardom he played *Richard III* as the usual opening or closing piece in his runs. This was not Shakespeare's play, but Colley Cibber's revision of it. And it concluded with a celebrated swordfight, into which Booth, like the father before him, was expected to throw himself with fiery abandon. Edwin Booth, however, worked long and hard to grow beyond that tradition, and he thus attained an exaggerated purity as a tragedian. His great role was *Hamlet* in a version that was not uncut Shakespeare but still took a long evening to perform. His great theater was Booth's Theatre in New York, an expensive and elaborate building explicitly advertised as a "temple" of refined art; it was so elaborate, in fact, and so far beyond the capacities of wide public appreciation, that Booth spent years on the road earning enough to keep up with its debts. Finally, Booth's enduring monument was a stately mansion in Gramercy Park— the building that he deeded to The Players, where actors might meet freely with other men of refinement. Nearby his statue as Hamlet stands in the park itself, a park fenced round against the intrusion of the unprivileged.

The December 1863 issue of *Harper's Magazine* tells a tale of three theaters that brings out this contrast and more. The editor narrates an evening tour of New York to show off the city to "a rustic friend" who has come to town. The pair begins this excursion at the Cooper Institute in "the great hall which was hung with banners, and devices, and festoons, and was as hot and uncomfortable as a place could be." Upon the stage are two orators, General John Cochrane (a former New York congressman) and the vice president of the United States. As Cochrane speaks, "vehemently declaiming and gesticulating," the packed crowd responds with "hearty cheers" and "intense interest." The editor remarks on this spectacle: "This before us was the government of the country. In public opinion, influenced by frank discussion, the true government of the nation lies. . . . It is by talk, by argument, by comparison, by enlightenment, by every means incessantly brought to bear upon public opinion, that we are governed. . . . Mr. Lincoln is the most successful and excellent of Presidents, because he has an instinctive perception, not of the whims and gusts of the rabble, but of the honest national desire."

The rustic friend expresses similar views, and they stroll on to Niblo's Theatre. Here Edwin Forrest is performing in another crammed house. The aisles, the stairs, the seats are full of people even though this must be the "thirty or forty somethingth night of the engagement," and though Forrest has been performing this way for generations. "Yet the crowd comes every night . . . because it delights in the representation, and shouts at it, and cries for more, and hastens and squeezes the next night to enjoy it all over again." The acting has been a standing joke for years: "We may call it the muscular school; the brawny art; the biceps aesthetics; the tragic calves; the bovine drama; rant, roar, and rigamarole; but what then?" It still delights the crowd. It still moves many to honest tears. It still expresses a well-worn American theatrical excellence. This night the play is *Damon and Pythias*. "And when, upon the temptation to escape, Pythias slapped his breast, and, pushing open the prison door with what may be termed 'a theatrical air,' roared out, 'Never, never!—death before dishonor!' the audience broke out into a storm of applause."

After one act, the two observers have seen enough and move on to the Winter Garden to see a different kind of acting. Here the play is *Othello*, but "the difference of the spectacle was striking. The house was comfortably full, not crowded. The air of the audience was that of refined attention rather than eager interest. Plainly it was a more cultivated and intellectual audience. . . . Pale, thin, intellectual, with long black hair and dark eyes, Shakespeare's Iago was perhaps never more adequately represented to the eye." And the actor is fully competent for "so quiet, and delicate, and subtle" a role. Yet there is a drawback to this performance, too, "a certain chilliness in the audience, which must have affected the actor. It was the attitude of an audience appreciative and expectant of fine points, but not irresistibly swept away." To the editor's regret, but the visitor's infinite amusement, the spell is broken when a long silence follows the smothering of Desdemona. At last a voice from the audience cries out, "What! is he a slaughtering on-her?" The audience laughs and claps and the play resumes and concludes.[6]

The date of this piece, to repeat, is 1863; and the new "intellectual" star who portrayed Iago at the Winter Garden was Edwin Booth. Lawrence Levine cites the essay very aptly to illustrate the extreme change in taste that occurred in the nineteenth-century theater; but his discussion omits two very important features, the visit to the Cooper Institute and the final break in the spell of the serious tragedy.[7] Taken as a whole, this essay celebrates old-fashioned Edwin Forrest tragedy as a wonderful American institution. It is allied on one side with the vigorous Lincoln-style democracy that hungers after crowded rooms and forceful debaters. It is contrasted on the other side with a drama so purified that it leaves a chill in the air, and needs to be broken by a loud and homely question of disbelief.

For Edwin Booth, the stakes in this drama between theaters must have been very high. To become this kind of Iago, he had to abandon older ways. Here, in fact, he is contrasted with the very man for whom his father named him, Edwin Forrest. In 1881, when he wrote his long letter about his younger brother, he was still working to endorse that contrast. Not only was his brother a notorious murderer, he was also an alter ego to be shunned, another Booth in a line of acting that was better obliterated. The terms "wild," "Quixotic," "crazy," have this edge of dismissal to them; they are hardly diagnostic, and terms of wildness and insanity were commonly used to describe and praise the old acting style of Kean, the elder Booth, and Edwin Forrest (Levine, pp. 38-39). "We were separated by professional engagements, which kept him mostly in the South": this is another line that has some basis in geography and timing, but much heavier significance about a realm of passion, patriotism, energy, and rusticity in the theater — a realm that Edwin needed to leave defeated and forgotten.

The deepest motives and character of John Wilkes Booth, the actor before 1865, may be lost beyond recovery forever. But certainly there were deep bonds and tensions between him and his father and brother, strains that ran much deeper than chronic melancholy and erratic flamboyance. The contrast and even enmity we have seen between theatrical traditions points to three further lines of identity these men came to terms with: their ambitions as American actors, their roots in an oral culture that celebrated republican political energy, and a symbolic separation between North and South that divided their loyalties as it divided their careers. These lines go far to explain how a very sane and talented man might have contemplated a daring act of assassination, and followed through in just the way John Wilkes Booth did.

Both Edwin and John were born to lives in the theater. Their father was an international star. He had rivaled Edmund Kean in London in his youth, before he came to America in 1821. Here he made his way almost immediately. For the next thirty years he was the leading American tragedian. Despite his frailties and eccentricities, partly because of them, he drew admiring audiences and held their loyalties. "Our father's name is a power — theatrical — in the land," John Wilkes told his sister in 1859, seven years after the old man's death. These words were engraved in her memory. "It is dower enough for any struggling actor" (*UB*, pp. 110-11).

The two older brothers were well-known actors and managers while Wilkes was still in his teens. Their sister Asia was married to another, their boyhood friend Jóhn Sleeper Clarke. And legendary theatrical people — Joseph Jefferson, Edwin Forrest, Laura Keene, and many others — were tied to the family through old adventures and well-tried associations.

But theatrical life in nineteenth-century America was a hard and haphazard business. It kept the finest actors on the road. There was no single center of American cultural life where theatrical companies could establish themselves for decades and compete to develop high standards of performance. There was no American equivalent of London or Paris. Single stars and small troupes moved from city to city, sometimes to join forces with settled stock companies, sometimes to make the best of chance opportunities. They performed a repertory of standard, familiar plays — Shakespearean comedies and tragedies along with melodramas or farces closely suited to the talents and fame of the leading actors. These roles were changed frequently; they often had to be changed on short notice to meet the limitations of a peculiar auditorium or catch the interest of a dwindling audience.

The Booths had to cope with these conditions, no matter how famous they became. Even at the height of their careers, they too were on the road. While John Wilkes was fleeing from Washington into southern Maryland and Virginia, in 1865, his relatives were to be found in several other cities. The oldest brother, Junius, was acting in Cincinnati. Edwin had just begun an engagement in Boston. Asia was with her husband in Philadelphia. And their mother was in New York at Edwin's home. Years earlier, when the great Junius was still alive, he had spent long months every year away from the house in Baltimore and the farm near Bel Air. In 1852 he took Edwin with him to San Francisco, after his son Junius urged him to come out and perform for the rich gold-rush settlements. But the profits turned out to be small compared to the hardships involved. The father gave up and returned, to die alone and exhausted aboard a Mississippi steamboat after making his way back and performing in New Orleans. The brothers plodded on through snowbound mining towns and competed with mixed success against other troupers in San Francisco. Edwin finally set out to pursue better fortune by joining Laura Keene's company bound for Australia — where he met with further disappointments.

Touring conditions were a demanding trial for beginners. There were sudden opportunities to take on enormous roles, and disasters just as sudden to leave an actor penniless and stranded. Frequent local notices could offer encouragement or devastating criticism. Troupes and partnerships could be solidified or broken apart by their travel into unknown territory.

For young John Wilkes, the family name combined with these circum-stances in a way different from the experiences of his brothers. By the time he reached the stage, they had inherited much of the father's powerful name and proved their own talents in many larger cities. Edwin had become a star in the North and East before 1860. Junius had pioneered in theaters farther west. Wilkes was free to carry the Booth name alone through the South, where he came to celebrity quickly, perhaps without proper training.

Booth's stage career has recently been documented by Gordon Samples, who provides a full list of his performances based on playbills and news-paper notices and reviews.[8] Much of his early experience was in the South, to be sure. For two seasons, 1858-59 and 1859-60, he worked as a member of the stock company in Richmond, Virginia (where his father first found work in America), and his first tour as a star began the following October, in a company that played in Columbus, Georgia, and Montgomery, Ala-bama. But from 1861 on, he starred in cities that remained with the Union. He had already tried to gain a name of his own. Early playbills usually list him as Mr. Wilks or Wilkes. But he had played opposite Edwin (in Baltimore and Richmond) under the name Booth, and it was as a Booth that he appeared on the final playbill in Montgomery and on every bill thereafter.

Perhaps his rush to stardom did him physical injury. An 1862 review in a Boston newspaper commented that he took on major roles "apparently, entirely ignorant of the main principles of elocution. We do not mean by this word merely enunciation, but the nature and proper treatment of the voice, as well. He ignores the fundamental principle of all vocal study and exercise — that the chest, and not the throat or mouth, should supply the sound necessary for singing or speaking." Later bouts with hoarseness led to cancellations and critical reviews late in the 1863-64 season; and in 1864-65, Booth played only three engagements. From this evidence Stanley Kimmel once argued that John Wilkes knew he was ruining his voice and so turned to plotting against Lincoln as his one remaining avenue to enduring fame.[9] But early celebrity had another definitely pernicious effect. It made John Wilkes the darling Booth of the South. Asia records a voice in the crowd, praising him at the brothers' joint appearance in *Julius Caesar* in November 1864:

In the densely packed theater I heard by my standing-place many comments on the merits of the brothers. One voice said delightedly, "*Our Wilkes* looks like a young god."
I turned to see a Southerner with eyes intently watching the play.

(*UB*, p. 122)

And in a more plangent tone, Asia records the young actor's sense of what such support might cost.

He felt it rather premature that Edwin should mark off for himself the North and the East, and leave the South where he no longer cared to go himself, to Wilkes. He felt that he had not had a chance in New York, and his Southern friends were fervid in their desire to make him prove himself in the cities of the North and East. He was having a wrong tuition in the ardent South, where even his errors were extolled and his successes magnified. The people loved him; he had never known privation or want, was never out of an engagement, while Edwin had had the rough schooling of poverty, hardship in far distant cities, struggles in his professional experience, fiercer struggles with himself. He had gone through the drudgery of his art through the fire of temptation, and he overcame and was victorious.

(*UB*, p. 112)

If the tone here accurately echoes John Wilkes's own voice, it bears witness to a clear awareness of a seductive danger. The South was all too easy and gratifying, all too ready to claim one Booth against the others for purely political reasons. Theatrical ambition combined with the Booth name and his older brothers' successes could push him toward alliance with the Confederacy.

This danger was heightened by the Booth family's reverence for libertarian heroes. It shows up in the family names through generations. The elder Junius's father was Richard Booth, an English lawyer who followed his son to America in 1822 and lived out his days on the family's Maryland farm. Richard claimed descent on his mother's side from the family of John Wilkes, the London agitator, and in 1777 young Richard (still in his teens) ran off from England to join the American Revolution. From Paris he and a cousin wrote a letter introducing themselves to the great Wilkes and asking him for a letter of recommendation to the Americans. Asia found this letter years later in the British Museum and copied its sentiments:

Our conduct has certainly been in some respects reprehensible, for too rashly putting in execution a project we had for a long time conceived. But as it was thro' an ardent desire to serve in the Glorious cause of Freedom, of which you have always been Fam'd for being the Strict and great Defender, we trust the request we are about to make will be paid regard to. As Englishmen, it may be urged that we are not altogether Justified in taking arms against our native Country, but we hope such a vague argument will have no weight with a Gentleman of your well-known abilities; for as that country has almost parted with all its Rights, which have been given up to the present Tyrannic Government, it must be thought the Duty of every true Briton to assist those who oppose oppression and lawless Tyranny.

(EYB, p. 5)

The two young adventurers even go on to compare themselves to "those illustrious worthys, Brutus and Cassius" (*EYB*, p. 5). John Wilkes immediately turned this letter over to Richard Booth's father, who fetched his son home again. But the other cousin did go to America and serve in the war. And according to Asia, her grandfather's long "love of Republicanism rendered him unpopular both as a lawyer and as a man. He kept a picture of General Washington in this drawing-room, before which he insisted that all who entered should bow with reverence" (*EYB*, p. 4). Perhaps the long reach of his influence can be seen in Edwin Booth's patriotic insistence on stretching the Stars and Stripes over his wife in childbirth in London in 1861, so that his one child would not be born under an alien flag.[10] A more serious influence is found in the family names. Richard's brother was named Wilkes Booth, and Richard named his two sons Junius Brutus and Algernon Sidney for similar heroes. Junius Brutus is of course the name of Marcus Brutus's legendary ancestor—the founder of republican Rome who drove out the last Tarquin king. Algernon Sidney was a seventeenth-century English republican leader, who was wounded at Marston Moor while fighting on the side of Parliament and later was executed for treason under Charles II.

These names may seem strange to a modern eye, but they reflect a common mood of late-eighteenth-century England. They celebrate resistance to despotism by literally impressing upon a new generation the heritage of hard-won British liberty. The names Junius and John Wilkes carried other, more immediate associations, too.

"Junius" was a celebrated name after 1769, not because of ancient Rome but because of ongoing British politics. It was the famous pseudonym of a writer whose identity has never been fully revealed. Safely hidden behind this name, he needled the ruling ministry and the king himself in a series of sixty letters to the London newspapers. The Junius letters created extra demand for the papers in which they appeared; they were widely reprinted; they provoked violent responses and futile efforts by the government to capture or suppress the author. And they had a direct political effect. "Junius' immediate political objective," writes his modern editor, "was the overthrow of the Grafton administration, which he regarded as dangerously subservient to the King. There can be little doubt that the stinging attacks upon Grafton helped to break his nerve and persuade him to resign."[11] In the longer term the Junius letters helped to open up new freedoms of the press. Junius was not a revolutionary, really; he argued for constitutional liberty against what he took to be particular recent corruptions and abuses. Leslie Stephen observes that Junius always leans on clear and conservative precedents: "The British Constitution is his ultimate appeal; Magna Charta and the Bill of Rights were to him what the Bible was to Chillingworth; there was no going behind them."[12] But the letters of Junius long stood as a monument of effective action against despotism.

John Wilkes was not just a name but a living symbol of the same principles. In fact he corresponded with Junius and was allied with him in many particular causes. Wilkes was a leader of London mobs, a daring political agitator. His most celebrated deeds included publishing a pointed attack on George III and then exploiting the persecution that followed. His paper No. 45 of the *North Briton* attacked the king's speech at the opening of Parliament and so gave the government a pretext for seizing his private papers and prosecuting him for libel. Wilkes fought back by suing the secretary of state for wrongful arrest and search — and he won. But he was pursued on other charges, expelled from Parliament, and declared an outlaw when he fled to Paris to escape conviction. Later, he had the nerve to return and run for Parliament for Middlesex, and when he was ejected he persisted in winning a series of reelections. "No. 45" and "Wilkes and Liberty" were common London slogans and graffiti. And the man himself was an unmistakable figure. Hogarth's famous print depicts the cross-eyed, ugly Wilkes leaning forward confidently from a parlor chair, with a liberty pole over his shoulder. His popularity in London assured him a steady seat in Parliament from 1774 to 1790, and he was elected lord mayor.

It should be stressed that both Junius and Wilkes were far from crude, though the latter enjoyed his coarser pleasures. They made a point of their own sophisticated elegance, especially when they could show up an adversary's stupidity, clumsiness, or grossness. They prided themselves on brilliant style as well as adherence to the highest political principles. At moments each quite explicitly saw himself in the role of a modern Brutus. In his first letter to Junius, Wilkes made the pointed comment, "I could plunge the patriot dagger in the heart of the tyrant of my country" (Cannon, ed., p. 418). Junius was just as ready to live up to his name. A public letter from William Draper challenged him in 1769: "People cannot bear any longer your *Lion's skin*, and the despicable *imposture* of the *old Roman name* which you have *affected*. For the future assume the name of some *modern* bravo and dark assassin: let your appellation have some affinity to your practice." By way of reply, Junius coolly footnoted the word "modern" when he reprinted this letter in 1772: "Was *Brutus* an *ancient* bravo and dark assassin; or does Sir W. D. think it criminal to stab a tyrant to the heart?" (Cannon, ed., p. 127)

Both Junius and Wilkes were also popular heroes in America at the time of the Revolution. Both seemed to have battled for constitutional liberty as forerunners of the American cause. In fact Arthur Lee, the Massachusetts agent in the early 1770s, sent letters to the London press as "Junius Americanus" and joined Wilkes in the Society of Supporters of the Bill of Rights. The American general Charles Lee was once identified as the author behind Junius; so was Thomas Paine (Cannon, ed., pp. 540n, 542n). Wilkes openly favored many of the Americans' arguments in the 1770s, even if he did refuse his young kinsmen's appeal for aid in rising in arms. Wilkes and Junius were not only among the most celebrated libertarians of their time, they also counted among the most dashing. They readily symbolized the constitutional principles for which Americans would shed blood, do away with monarchy, and establish a new republic over an extent of territory unmatched since ancient Rome.

One other name also fascinated the American Booths. At some point in his career, Edwin paid to have his ancestors traced. He hoped to find a link back to Barton Booth, the celebrated actor of the early eighteenth century. In his time (1681-1733) this Booth was a leading Shakespearean on the London stage, famous as Lear, Othello — and Brutus. He was also a manager of Drury Lane at the same time as another well-known actor named Robert Wilks. Barton Booth leapt into prominence when he took the starring role in Joseph Addison's *Cato* (1713), and in that role he figured in a well-known political legend. *Cato* is a blank-verse tragedy about the uncle of Marcus Brutus who died on his sword rather than submit to

Caesar. The play was first produced during a time of high political tension in London, and the Tory minister Bolingbroke used it to bring off a dramatic masterstroke. He collected a purse of fifty guineas from the boxes one night and made an elaborate gesture of presenting it to Booth for "defending the cause of liberty so well against a perpetual dictator."[13]

Edwin Booth's genealogists could not establish a link to Barton Booth, to his regret. But that name along with the names of John Wilkes, Algernon Sidney, and Junius Brutus continued to live on in the family. Junius Brutus Booth, Jr., remarried in 1867 and had four sons—named Junius Brutus Booth III, Algernon C. Booth, Sydney Barton Booth, and Barton J. Booth.[14]

Plutarch and Shakespeare made much of the legend that Brutus was spurred on to action against Caesar by reminders of his great ancestor.

> His friends and countrymen . . . did openly call and procure him to do [what] he did. For, under the image of his ancestor Junius Brutus, that drave the kings out of Rome, they wrote: "Oh that it pleased the gods thou wert now alive, Brutus." And again: "That thou wert here among us now." His tribunal, or chair, where he gave audience during the time he was Praetor, was full of such bills: "Brutus, thou art asleep, and art not Brutus indeed."[15]

So John Wilkes Booth might have heard echoes within his name. Sidney, Junius, Brutus, John Wilkes, Booth: here were five names, each renowned for "defending the cause of Liberty against a perpetual dictator." He might well have asked if he were John Wilkes Booth indeed.

Finally, the Booths were well known as actors who had sprung from homely American roots in Maryland. The parents had kept a home in Baltimore and John Wilkes had some advantages of private schooling; but the family also kept a farm about twenty-five miles to the northeast, near Bel Air. It was at this farm that nine of the ten Booth children were born, and there John Wilkes Booth spent his boyhood after his father's death in 1852. By then the older brothers had traveled far away. Johnnie was left at the age of fourteen as the oldest male, to help manage a farm and farm laborers, in a slave state.

Asia records a deep struggle he went through in reconciling two family traits even to sit down with white workers:

> The first evidence of an undemocratic feeling in Wilkes was shown when we were expected to sit down with our hired workmen. It was the custom for members of the family to dine and sup with the white men who did the harvesting. Wilkes had a struggle with his

pride and knew not which to abide by, his love of equality and
brotherhood, or that southern reservation which jealously kept the
white laborer from free association with his employer or his superior.
His father would not have hesitated an instant, nor would Richard
Booth, the rebel-patriot grandfather, have considered the matter twice.
The difference between the impassioned self-made Republican and
the native-born southern American is wide. One overleaps restraint
by his enthusiasm, desiring to cast off at a swoop the trammels of a
former allegiance, and is over eager to fraternize with all men; but
the other cautiously creates for himself a barrier called respect, with
which he fences off familiarity and its concomitant evils. This made
the master a god in the South, to be either loved or feared.

(UB, p. 63)

Wilkes resolved the problem by a compromise. He ceded the head of the
table to the oldest workman and seated himself among the others, but he
never allowed his mother and sisters to eat with the men. Asia records
the consequence: "We were not a popular family with our white laborers,
because, as they said, 'They'd heer'd we had dirty British blood, and being
mixed up with Southern ideas and niggers made it dirtier'" (UB, p. 65).

Asia herself gives vent to a resentment against "that grommeling of
disaffection which would ultimately drive out black labor" (UB, p. 65).
She recounts several admiring stories of Wilkes terrorizing or fooling "the
darkies," slipping out to Know-Nothing meetings, or thrashing an insolent
sharecropper. The impression is clear that John Wilkes spent his adoles-
cence in the 1850s learning both the hardships and the swagger of a
southern farmer. The story comes to a climax in a sharp exchange between
brother and sister during the war. John Wilkes began it:

> "The time will come, whether conquered or conqueror, when the
> braggart North will groan at not being able to swear they fought the
> South man for man. If the North conquer us it will be by numbers
> only, not by native grit, not pluck, and not by devotion."
> "If the North conquers us—we are of the North," I said.
> "Not I, not I!" he said excitedly. "So help me holy God! my soul,
> life, and possessions are for the South."
> "Why not go fight for her, then? Every Marylander worthy the
> name is fighting her battles."

(UB, p. 115)

Not every Marylander was fighting for the South. Maryland remained
a Union state; "We are of the North," Asia rightly protests here. But her

sharp retort still has its sting. Maryland was a torn state in the 1860s: a slave state still allied with the North, poised between Virginia and Pennsylvania, surrounding the District of Columbia. It was notorious that Lincoln had dodged around Baltimore in 1861 and come into Washington in disguise on his way to the inauguration, for fear of an assassination plot. Later that year the president seemed to violate the Constitution when he approved the military arrests of Maryland secessionists.

One of these, named John Merryman, was detained at Fort McHenry in defiance of a writ of habeas corpus, and even the chief justice of the Supreme Court ruled that such detention was flagrantly unconstitutional. "I have exercised all the power which the Constitution and laws confer upon me," wrote Chief Justice Taney (when he decided the case on circuit), "but that power has been resisted by a force too strong for me to overcome. . . . I shall therefore order all the proceedings in this case, with my opinion, to be filed and recorded . . . and direct the clerk to transmit a copy . . . to the President of the United States. It will then remain for that high officer, in fulfillment of his constitutional obligation to 'take care that the laws be faithfully executed' to determine what measure he will take to cause the civil process of the United States to be respected and enforced."[16] Lincoln's officers continued to ignore habeas corpus writs, nevertheless, following his claim that the government had to take extraordinary measures to control the corridor between the North and its capital. In his first message to Congress Lincoln explained that the Constitution authorized such measures "in cases of rebellion or invasion," and he asked pointedly: "Are all the laws, *but one*, to go unexecuted, and the government itself to go to pieces, lest that one be violated?"[17]

Taney's celebrated decision bore its own taint, to be sure. A modern historian comments: "Taney's sympathies were with the Confederacy. He favored peaceable separation, considered the war a descent into madness, detested Republicans as a class, and regarded the Lincoln administration as a hateful despotism." Still, the law was on Taney's side, and a later decision of the full Supreme Court denied the strict legality of what Lincoln had done.[18]

It was thus over Maryland that Lincoln's legitimacy as a constitutional president was early called into question. Was he a constitutional commander, observing the letter of the law, with further justification in an emergency? Or was he a tyrant, defying even the explicit judgment of the chief justice, that Maryland was a civil state, not an invaded or rebellious territory, and that it was for Congress, not the president, to decide whether habeas corpus could be suspended? Taney charged that Lincoln had gone even further in violating the Constitution. After reviewing the facts in this case and all precedents and analogies in American history, the chief justice concluded that "the military authority in this case . . . has, by force of arms, thrust aside the judicial authorities and officers to whom the Constitution has confined the power and duty of interpreting and administering the laws, and substituted a military government in its place" (Commager, 1: 400-401).

In Maryland these questions were not only argued but felt. The early strategy of the war seemed to turn on the capture of either Washington or Richmond, and Maryland remained a battleground to the end. The felt anguish of that time and place survives in "Maryland, My Maryland," the state anthem. Its words were composed in 1861 and set to the tune of the German song "O Tannenbaum" to become a popular Confederate song. James Ryder Randall, a man about John Wilkes Booth's age, had found his way from Baltimore to a teaching job in Louisiana after a bout with pneumonia. In April 1861 he heard of bloodshed when the Sixth Massachusetts Regiment had been attacked and had fired on a Baltimore crowd. One of Randall's school classmates had been wounded, and he stayed up through the night to compose a call to arms in verse.

This poem was published in a New Orleans newspaper and widely recopied. It was set to music in Baltimore by Jennie and Hetty Cary, then set to "O Tannenbaum" by Charles Ellerbrock, and finally carried to a publisher by Rebecca Lloyd Nicholson. Because her father was a known Union man, Nicholson "dared to do it when others feared confinement in Fort McHenry or in federal prisons."[19] The Nicholsons were distant relatives of Francis Scott Key and direct descendants of the first publisher of "The Star Spangled Banner" — another song born of military actions in Maryland. The original cover of "Maryland, My Maryland" bore the Maryland coat of arms and the credits, "Written by a Baltimorean in Louisiana. Music Adapted and Arranged by C. E."[20] The song was later parodied, and its words were recast to reflect on rebel threats against the North. But Randall's original verses call bitterly for vengeance against the tyranny of Lincoln.

> The despot's heel is on thy shore,
> Maryland!
> His torch is at thy temple door,
> Maryland!
> Avenge the patriotic gore

That flecked the streets of Baltimore,
And be the battle queen of yore,
Maryland! My Maryland!

Hark to a wand'ring son's appeal,
Maryland!
My mother State! to thee I kneel,
Maryland!
For life and death, for woe and weal,
Thy peerless chivalry reveal
And gird thy beauteous limbs with steel,
Maryland! My Maryland!

Dear Mother! burst the tyrant's chain,
Maryland!
Virginia should not call in vain,
Maryland!
She meets her sisters on the plain —
"*Sic semper!*" 'tis the proud refrain
That baffles minions back again,
Maryland! My Maryland![21]

"The despot's heel is on thy shore . . . Avenge the patriotic gore . . . Burst the tyrant's chain . . . '*Sic Semper!*' 'tis the proud refrain." These are words John Wilkes Booth could not have escaped hearing often, and they were reinforced at least once by a sister's taunt: "Every Marylander worthy the name is fighting her battles."

Exactly how Booth became involved in conspiracies against Lincoln has long been a matter of controversy, and no doubt it will be argued long into the future. What his exact connections were with other Confederate agents; how deliberately or expertly he laid plans to capture Lincoln or kill him; what he did in his travels to Montreal, his projected travels to Richmond, and his movements past Union lines on his way to distant engagements — all these have remained baffling questions.[22] But the explanation that he was mad, a wild incarnation of Booth eccentricities, will not do. He may just as well have been an embodiment of Booth sanities and strengths.

What even Asia records as "wild tirades" of his "distracted brain" have their own logic as anguished outbursts against what many others saw and feared in Lincoln. To thousands of people, north and south, Lincoln was far from an admirable statesman. He was often attacked, caricatured, criticized, vilified, and mocked. There were public calls for resistance to his usurpations of power, even for his murder. After the assassination there were members of his own cabinet who felt not mourning but relief. There were many sane northerners who openly rejoiced.[23]

It is against this background that one must read Asia's account of her brother's "tirade." She had pleaded with him not to go south again.

> "Why, where *should* I go then?" he said, opening his eyes wide in astonishment, as if the South held his heartstrings. Then he sang low and distinctly a wild parody, each verse ending with a rhyme to a year, then, "In 1865 when Lincoln shall be king."
>
> I said, "Oh, not that—that will *never* come to pass!"
>
> "No, by God's mercy," he said, springing to his feet. "Never *that!*" Then he whispered fiercely, "That Sectional Candidate should never have been President, the votes were *doubled* to seat him, he was smuggled through Maryland to the White House. Maryland is true to the core—every mother's son. Look at the cannon on the heights of Baltimore. It needed just that to keep her quiet. This man's appearance, his pedigree, his coarse low jokes and anecdotes, his vulgar similes, and his frivolity, are a disgrace to the seat he holds. Other brains rule the country. *He* is made the tool of the North, to crush out, or try to crush out slavery, by robbery, rapine, slaughter and bought armies. He is walking in the footprints of old John Brown, but no more fit to stand with that rugged old hero—Great God! no. John Brown was a man inspired, the grandest character of this century! [As it happened, Booth had personally witnessed Brown's execution after the raid on Harper's Ferry.] *He* is Bonaparte in one great move, that is, by overturning this blind Republic and making himself a king. This man's re-election which will follow his success, I tell you—will be a reign!
>
> (*UB*, 123-24)

So far the language may be heated, but it is coherent. Maryland was under military domination. Lincoln had gone around Baltimore to the White House. The president was widely thought of as low, coarse, vulgar, unqualified, and worst of all ambitious to overthrow the Constitution. The lines that follow go beyond such bounds.

> "The subjects—bastard subjects—of other countries, apostates, are eager to overturn this government. You'll see—you'll see—that *re-election* means *succession*. His kin and friends are in every place of office already. Trust the songs of the people—they are the bards, the troubadours. Who makes these songs if not the people? 'Vox populi' for

ever! These false-hearted, unloyal foreigners it is, who would glory in
the downfall of the Republic — and that by a half-breed too, a man
springing from the ashes of old Assanothime Brown, a false president
for yearning for kingly succession as hotly as ever did Ariston."

(*UB*, pp. 124-25)

But without hearing these words directly, and knowing their speaker much
better than we ever can, it is impossible to know how they were meant.
They may have sprung from an outbreak of chronic, congenital madness;
or a momentary burst of passion, tension, and war hysteria; or from a
practiced actor's maneuver to deceive even his sister about his state of
mind.

As an actor Booth was loved and fostered by the South. As a son and
grandson of immigrant republicans, he was brought up in a living American tradition that applauded active, conspicuous resistance to tyrants. As
an orphaned adolescent on a Maryland farm, he was imbued with the
values and passions of his slaveholding neighbors. And around him were
a hundred echoing public pronouncements that Lincoln was violating the
Constitution. These conditions might be urged as sufficient to lead him
into his conspiracy, without any tincture of madness. A person in his
position might well have looked around like Hamlet at a world gone mad.

> The time is out of joint — O cursed spite
> That ever I was born to set it right!
>
> (1.5.188-89)

A further cruel coincidence worked upon this particular mind and
passion. Just as John Wilkes Booth came of age and laid claim to his
inheritance as a dramatic star, the North became ranged against the South
on the field of battle, and one conception of theater confronted another
within his own family. The older, well-loved tradition of tragic entertainment was still alive, still understood as a dramatic counterpart to free and
responsive American government. But Edwin Forrest was growing old, and
Edwin Booth was moving in a new direction, toward a cool, intellectual,
lofty, privileged art. John Wilkes Booth quickly attained fame, glamor,
money, and critical praise as an actor. But in 1865 he completed his form
of art in one further final step. In one aspect he acted like Hamlet, with
a cunning improvisational play within a play. In another he played the
part of the most critical common spectator, and responded to the modern
stage by hurling a dangerous missile down from the gallery. The explosive
missile he had to hurl was himself.

5

The Tragic Lincoln

"*L*INCOLN is the supremely tragic figure of a tragic war, and not only because of the way his life ended. He rose to the presidency from deeper obscurity than any of his predecessors, only to find himself in the grip of a deadly historical irony. That is, his own unexpected and dazzling personal triumph in 1860 had signalized—indeed, to some degree had caused—the onset of national calamity. For a man sensitive enough to perceive the irony and its bloody implications, there was bound to be, always, sorrow on the bosom of the earth." These words conclude a short essay on Lincoln's moral depth, written by Don E. Fehrenbacher, a sensitive and seasoned modern scholar of Lincoln's life and career.[1] The essay points out Lincoln's conscious acceptance of responsibility for war, and its destruction, his deep questioning and probing of the will of God and the freedom of man. In a more recent essay, Fehrenbacher suggests that Lincoln's tragic power also springs from his representative role in a great national catastrophe. He quotes with approval a passage from the New York *Herald* published soon after the assassination: "He may not have been, and perhaps was not, our most perfect product in any one branch of mental or moral education, but taking him for all in all, the very noblest impulses, peculiarities and aspirations of our whole people—what may be called our continental idiosyncracies—

were more collectively and vividly reproduced in his genial and yet answering nature than in that of any other public man of whom our chronicles bear record." Fehrenbacher goes on: "The national myth had for the most part celebrated *achievement*, such as the winning of independence and the conquest of the wilderness. To that national tradition the Lincoln legend now added the element of high tragedy. In Lincoln's tragic death, as in the lines of sadness etched on his face, there was epitomized all the pain and sorrow of a nation's descent into the self-destructive violence of civil war."[2]

These lines call Lincoln a supremely tragic figure with a careful and precise sense of language. What is more, Fehrenbacher argues that Lincoln fully understood his tragic role. He draws together several bits of evidence about the president's reading, playgoing, and engagement with actors and fellow spectators, to suggest that Lincoln learned tragedy directly from Shakespeare; he even surmises what Lincoln may have seen in himself in comparison with some great Shakespearean figures, including Claudius in *Hamlet*, Macbeth, and Richard III. It was "to some indeterminable extent and in some intuitive way," he admits; but "Lincoln seems to have assimilated the substance of the plays into his own experience and deepening sense of tragedy" (p. 158).

Any view of Lincoln as tragic, however, has its perils. It is a view inevitably colored by the facts of Lincoln's involvement in the Civil War and his own sudden death by violence. What Lincoln's consciousness was like up to the moment of death we can only surmise and infer, and we are all obliged to frame it now with a heavy frame of black. There is no denying that Lincoln pondered Shakespeare, thought deeply and in pain about the cosmic issues of the Civil War, and transmuted his experience into magnanimous speeches and gestures of enduring power. But there is also no denying that Lincoln did other things, too. The record of his Shakespearean experiences in particular reveals that he took in tragedy, and lived through tragedy, with an understanding different from the one we may impose upon him. Two famous incidents — both cited in detail by Fehrenbacher — disclose a Lincoln much livelier and less solemn than "high tragedy" allows.

The first is his well-known letter to the Shakespearean actor, James Henry Hackett, acknowledging Hackett's gift of his book, *Notes and Comments upon Certain Plays and Actors of Shakespeare*. This letter contains Lincoln's fullest comment on Shakespeare, and it figures in a complex chain of events. Hackett had sent his book to the president in March 1863, but Lincoln did not acknowledge it until August 17. He then apologized for his delay and made amends with this full paragraph:

> For one of my age, I have seen very little of the drama. The first presentation of Falstaff I ever saw was yours here, last winter or spring. Perhaps the best compliment I can pay is to say, as I truly can, I am very anxious to see it again. Some of Shakespeare's plays I have never read; while others I have gone over perhaps as frequently as any unprofessional reader. Among the latter are Lear, Richard Third, Henry Eighth, Hamlet, and especially Macbeth. I think nothing equals Macbeth. It is wonderful. Unlike you gentlemen of the profession, I think the soliloquy in Hamlet commencing "O, my offence is rank" surpasses that commencing "To be, or not to be." But pardon this small attempt at criticism. I should like to hear you pronounce the opening speech of Richard the Third. Will you not soon visit Washington again? If you do please call and let me make your personal acquaintance.
>
> (LCW, 6: 392-93)

Hackett proudly had this letter printed as a broadside, and it was recopied in many newspapers. Fehrenbacher quotes the New York *Herald* of September 17: "Mr. Lincoln's genius is wonderfully versatile. No department of human knowledge seems to be unexplored by him. . . . It only remained for him to cap the climax of popular astonishment and admiration by showing himself to be a dramatic critic of the first order, and the greatest and most profound of the army of Shakespearean commentators" (Fehrenbacher, p. 157). To a modern eye this may look like a contemporary expression of praise, but it was well understood as sarcasm at the time. Hackett wrote a contrite note to Lincoln in November. To his contemporaries, in other words, Mr. Lincoln did not seem a particularly acute or profound student of Shakespeare.

Lincoln's letter itself reflects a mixed appreciation of Shakespeare's plays. It was not until he saw Hackett that Lincoln saw Falstaff. Though he mentions rereading three or four tragedies he also fails to mention many others. And his attention is evidently focused here on passages rather than tragic designs. Fehrenbacher notes that to complete this episode with Hackett, Lincoln invited him to the White House and then went three nights out of four to see him as Falstaff in the *Henry* plays and *The Merry Wives of Windsor*.[3] This is hardly evidence of a mind intent on tragedy. It rather makes Lincoln sound like an ordinary theatergoer of his time, brought

up to appreciate good oratory and declamation, fond of a variety of entertainments including many kinds of plays by Shakespeare, and ready to
applaud an Edwin Forrest as loudly as an Edwin Booth. On November 9,
1863, he even went to Ford's Theatre to see John Wilkes Booth in the
melodrama, *The Marble Heart*. His young secretary John Hay recorded
the performance as "rather tame than otherwise."[4]

Another incident very late in Lincoln's life seems to cast a more somber
glow over his reading of Shakespeare, if not over his playgoing. "In Lincoln's
view," Fehrenbacher writes, "no other play could rival *Macbeth*, and he
was drawn especially to the scene following the murder of Duncan. Six
days before his own death, while steaming back up the Potomac after a
visit to captured Richmond, he read and reread this passage to his companions, pausing to expatiate on Shakespeare's discerning portrayal of the
murderer's mind" (Fehrenbacher, p. 160).

This story in its original form seems even more uncanny in foreshad-
owing a mighty death. This account was written by one of the small
party that was with Lincoln aboard the *River Queen*:

> On Sunday, April 9th, we were steaming up the Potomac. That
> whole day the conversation dwelt upon literary subjects. Mr. Lincoln
> read to us for several hours passages taken from Shakespeare. Most
> of these were from "Macbeth," and, in particular, the verses which
> follow *Duncan's* assassination. I cannot recall this reading without
> being awed at the remembrance, when *Macbeth* becomes king after
> the murder of *Duncan*, he falls a prey to the most horrible torments
> of mind.
>
> Either because he was struck by the weird beauty of these verses,
> or from a vague presentiment coming over him, Mr. Lincoln paused
> here while reading, and began to explain to us how true a description
> of the murderer that one was; when, the dark deed achieved, its
> tortured perpetrator came to envy the sleep of his victim; and he read
> over again the same scene.[5]

Here indeed is a penetrating meditation on tragedy and in particular on
the torments that await a usurper or a political assassin.

But this account does not stop here. It goes on with further sinister
foreshadowings:

> Evening came on quickly. Passing before Mount Vernon, I remember
> saying to him: "Mount Vernon and Springfield, the memories of
> Washington and your own, those of the revolutionary and civil wars;
> these are the spots and names America shall one day equally honor."

This remark appeared to call him to himself. "Springfield!" answered he. "How happy, four years hence, will I be to return there in peace and tranquility!"

Arrived at the Potomac wharf, our party was forced to disperse. Mr. and Mrs. Lincoln, Senator Sumner, and myself drove home in the same carriage. We were nearing Washington when Mrs. Lincoln, who had hitherto remained silently looking at the town a short distance off, said to me: "That city is filled with our enemies." On hearing this the President raised his arm and somewhat impatiently retorted, "Enemies! We must never speak of that." This was on the evening of April 9th.

Here again, there is too much evidence to make Lincoln a convincing figure, a man prophetically finding his own reflection in Shakespeare's pages. This account was evidently written with the assassination weighing on the writer's mind (it is the final incident of this memoir), and every detail is laden with ominous significance.

Lincoln may well have read aloud and meaningfully to his friends aboard the *River Queen*. He no doubt read Shakespeare silently to himself and aloud to others on apt occasions during his presidency. This passage fits easily with many other memories from his aides and acquaintances, recording his striking recollections of Shakespeare in their presence.[6] But such recollections have come to light after the assassination, and they carry enough pathos to obliterate their original life and flavor.

This account of *Macbeth* on the *River Queen* mentions that Senator Charles Sumner was one of the group traveling with Lincoln on April 9. And Sumner's recent biographer sees a very different significance in Lincoln's behavior that day. "Once again Lincoln exhibited his skill in the delicate art of managing the Senator," he writes, noting that this was their last meeting. "He steered conversation away from the controversial issues of reconstruction and did not discuss his decision to permit the reconvening of the Virginia Confederate legislature in order to take that state out of the war. Instead, he reminisced in a mellow, retrospective tone about the events of the past four years and once again neutralized Sumner's anticipated opposition by talk of cabinet appointments." How ingenious of Lincoln, then, to read aloud from Shakespeare as the *River Queen* thumped along on the Potomac. What better way to keep conversation neutral and even flattering to the proudly cultivated senator from Massachusetts, whom Mary Lincoln described on this day as "our stately, dignified Mr. Sumner."[7]

Sumner's own records add yet another dimension to this story by providing a contrasting incident a few days earlier. On March 17 Sumner came to the president with a long opinion in favor of some constituents who had been imprisoned and fined by a court-martial; he persuaded Lincoln to hear him out that very night, returned at eleven o'clock, and pleaded his case until well after midnight. By nine the next morning Lincoln had prepared and signed a full annulment of the court's judgment. But Sumner's third-person account adds a further incident at this point, a touch "as original as anything in the life of Henry IV of France, or of a Lacedaemonian king." Lincoln took time to read out the satirical letters in dialect of a crude pro-southern extremist.

> As Mr. Sumner was making an abstract of the indorsement for communication by telegraph to the anxious parties, the President broke into quotation from Petroleum V. Nasby; and seeing that his visitor was less at home than himself in this patriotic literature, he said, "I must initiate you," and then repeated with enthusiasm the message he had sent to the author: "For the genius to write these things I would gladly give up my office!" Then rising and turning to a standing-desk behind, he opened it, and took out a pamphlet collection of the letters already published, which he proceeded to read aloud, evidently enjoying it much. For the time he seemed to forget the case he had just decided, and Presidential duties. This continued more than twenty minutes, when Mr. Sumner, thinking there must be many at the door waiting to see the President on graver matters, took advantage of a pause, and, thanking him for the lesson of the morning, left. Some thirty persons, including senators and representatives, were in the anteroom as he passed out. Though with the President much during the intervening days before his death, this was the last business Mr. Sumner transacted with him.[8]

Here is another final incident, recalled as a prelude to Lincoln's death. Here is another moment of Lincoln reading aloud, and to the same Mr. Sumner. But there is not solemnity here but exasperating levity: Lincoln indulging in raw-boned humor while others with "graver matters" try to get on with their business or wait in forced idleness beyond the door. Was Lincoln deliberately teasing "our stately, dignified Mr. Sumner," in return for his earnest pestering until late hours? If so, he seems to have made amends by taking him along to Grover's Theatre that night, the president's next-to-last visit to any theater.

This story, too, rings true to what we know about Lincoln. It matches his long reading of Artemus Ward to his cabinet before announcing the

Emancipation Proclamation. It also underscores his notorious laughter and joke telling in the midst of wartime disasters and despair. A cartoon in *Harper's Weekly* for January 3, 1863, showed Columbia angrily confronting the president, at the doorway of the War Department, and demanding an explanation for thousands slain. Lincoln, flanked by General Halleck and Secretary Stanton, answers, "This reminds me of a little joke." The indignant matron replies: "Go tell your joke at Springfield."[9]

These two parallel incidents of Lincoln's reading aloud do not prove that Lincoln was tragic. But they also do not prove that he was too frivolous to be tragic. They rather show that he was a complex living person and not a literary character. He could, and can, become tragic only by a very selective arrangement of details and circumstances from history.

Moreover, these stories show that Lincoln lived in a space between two different conceptions of tragedy, the same poles that we have seen separating Edwin and John Wilkes Booth. Lincoln's fondness for the theater as entertainment and his liking for homespun humor set him comfortably in the old-fashioned theater of a miscellaneous playbill and the muscular histrionics of Edwin Forrest. As we saw the *Harper's* editor remarking in 1863, this theater was the close counterpart of Lincoln's political debates and oratory before crowds of attentive common citizens. But his private reading and his alert companionship with refined intellectual men like Charles Sumner place him in another line as well, in the hushed polite theater of Edwin Booth and of Shakespeare at his most serious. It is this highly tragic Lincoln that addresses us, too, in the fineness of his greatest speeches and messages.

To make Lincoln highly tragic thus takes an effort to suppress the awkward, homely, joke-cracking politician, an effort much like Edwin Booth's silence and evasions concerning his brother. Yet the tragic Lincoln has long held a place in the American memory, and it seems almost inevitable that he should. Part of this work of suppression is simply a necessity of history. To understand anyone from the past, we have to select some details and forget or subordinate others. We hold on best to details arranged in a pattern, and the pattern of tragedy serves to fit Lincoln together with the Civil War as a meaningful part of our heritage. It also holds together hundreds of other details about such things as Lincoln's simplicity among common people, his many acts of generosity, and his reading of tragedies by Shakespeare. Much more of our collective suppression was accomplished by the sharp, hard fact of the assassination. No one wants to speak evil of the dead, and Booth's murder transformed

Lincoln from a controversial president to a pitiable victim, a martyr, an American demigod. As Fehrenbacher very perceptively notices, the assassination did not completely transform people's opinions, but it suddenly and powerfully brought out Lincoln's deeper qualities and forced even his harshest critics to mention his name in a different tone (Fehrenbacher, p. 203).

The question to ask about the Lincoln tragedy is not whether or not it is historically substantiated, but what deep significance it still carries. To pick up the question we developed in the opening chapter—what is the epiphany of law to be glimpsed by seeing Lincoln as a tragic figure? The deepest hazard of magnifying Lincoln under the lens of tragedy is that, like Caesar long before him, he can seem a martyr to some or a tyrant to others, and then be used by yet others to consolidate and justify an enduring national sense of "what is and must be." There is more than one deep version of the Lincoln tragedy, and it behooves us to measure them against one another.

Fehrenbacher's essays sum up and finely state a long historical tradition of appreciating Lincoln: He is the supreme hero through whom we see into what is deep, enduring, and just in American law. In part, American law is literally the American legal code, consisting of the Declaration of Independence, the Constitution, and all federal laws and court decisions. American law, in another sense, is what is and must happen in America, or especially in America. Lincoln's career brilliantly illuminates both these ideas of law. He is the statesman whose tenacity, forbearance, and legal wisdom held the Union together through and beyond the Civil War. And he is the man whose life experience between 1809 and 1865 was a rise from the earthiness of poverty and obscurity on the frontier to the heights of political power and transcendental understanding. These two versions of law overlap and merge in Lincoln; they both reflect the same ideals of human equality of opportunity; democratic, participatory government; prosperity as a reward for merit; and resolute defense of national integrity. The passages quoted at the beginning of this chapter show that Fehrenbacher has celebrated this understanding of Lincoln now, and found it clearly stated in 1865. It derives, in fact, from Lincoln's own explicit statements in the 1850s and 1860s of what the Constitution meant, why he was running for office, and what policies he must pursue in the war and thereafter.

But as Thomas J. Pressly once pointed out very extensively, this Lincoln orthodoxy is only one of many versions of the Civil War and Lincoln's place in history.[10] And carried to its fully felt extreme, it is an orthodoxy indeed. It enshrines Lincoln as not only a hero but a prophet or a divinity. His deep reading of Shakespeare gives way to his deep reading of the Bible as the mental and moral discipline that fitted him to interpret and defend the Constitution. He is the son in whom the Founding Fathers were well pleased; the haunting, transfigured presence of "The Battle Hymn of the Republic"; the American word of law made flesh, that dwelt among us. On Good Friday 1865 he was put to a lingering death, but he is still alive in his words. They line the walls of his temple in the capital. Our children recite them as our creed. His image circulates everywhere on our humblest coin.

To almost any American historian, the Lincoln of history is the Lincoln made numinous by this myth. This is the figure we study in school, learn about anyhow in childhood, and find everywhere as a patriotic symbol. But there have long been other thoughtful accounts of Lincoln written by observers who stood apart from America. Two in particular serve to filter out much of this blinding glory. After the war, the vice president of the Confederacy wrote a long defense of the southern cause, including a critique of Lincoln's role in the 1860s. And decades later a British writer published a well-balanced biography to bring out Lincoln's political contribution to the modern world. Both these writers have their reasons for seeing Lincoln as a public figure in a dangerous office. Both have their own articulate, rooted principles which they oppose to his highest ideals. Both regard him finally as the leader of a very foreign country. Yet these writers see him, too — though for different reasons — as the protagonist in a great modern tragedy.

To the vice president of the Confederate States of America, Lincoln was a well-meaning but unseeing man who undermined the original Constitution in a disastrous and needless war. This was Alexander Hamilton Stephens of Liberty Hall in Georgia, a man with a name as remarkably patriotic as the Booths'. His long, heavily documented reflection on the war might almost serve as a manifesto after the fact for the assassination.

Stephens could claim a number of grounds for writing with personal authority about the events of the 1860s. He had participated directly in the Confederate government, had long represented the South in Congress, and had known Lincoln personally as a fellow congressman in the 1840s. On one celebrated occasion Lincoln wrote his law partner that "Mr. Stephens of Georgia, a little, slim, pale-faced, consumptive man . . . has just concluded the very best speech, of an hour's length, I ever heard. My old, withered, dry eyes, are full of tears yet."[11] Stephens had renewed his direct acquaintance with Lincoln as late as February 1865. He met him at Hampton Roads on a secret embassy to discuss exchanging prisoners and possibly ending the war. Stephens still exerts an appeal to a modern reader as a serious southerner with his own consistent principles. He was a career statesman of a kind akin to Jefferson or Madison or Clay or Calhoun. He patiently collected documents and vigilantly analyzed the points of his adversaries' arguments, until he could trace the course of large political disputes and understandings through many decades. And he persisted in his career through pain and sorrow. He was, as Lincoln describes him, little, frail, and prematurely aged by chronic ailments. At war's end he was held in Boston harbor for four months, two of them in a dank prison cell, in suspense about whether he would be tried for treason. (Jefferson Davis was still facing charges as a conspirator in Lincoln's murder.) Yet he survived that and many other crippling ordeals. After his political disability was removed in 1872 he went back to spend another decade in Congress. Then at the age of seventy he ran for governor of Georgia and died in office. By that time he was a crippled, muffled, carefully wrapped bundle, still possessed of burning eyes. Edmund Wilson concludes, "It was as if he had shrunk to pure principle, abstract, incandescent, indestructible."[12]

During his years out of office after the war, Stephens attempted to establish an indestructible legacy in print. He composed his two thick volumes under a title equally ponderous: *A Constitutional View of the Late War Between the States; its Causes, Character, Conduct and Results. Presented in a Series of Colloquies at Liberty Hall.*[13] The whole work runs to just under 1,500 pages, including twenty-seven appendixes. Its main argument is that secession was an important constitutional right, guaranteed to the individual states and well understood by the founders and the statesmen of the early republic. What the North called a rebellion or civil war was therefore properly a war between the states. And its central issue was not slavery but centralized power. The epigraph on the title page reads, "Times change and men often change with them, but principles never!" Stephens summarized the important principles in his Introduction. "The conflict in principle arose from different and opposing ideas as to the nature of what is known as the central government. The contest was between those who held it to be strictly Federal in its character, and those who maintained that it was thoroughly National. It was a strife between the principles of Federation, on the one side, and Centralism, or Consolidation, on the other" (1: 10).

Stephens contends (to his own satisfaction, he proves) that the war was initiated, conducted, and won by the North in a movement that overturned the original federal character of the Constitution. We need not follow his argument in full detail; perhaps only a few hundred readers ever have. It is a meticulous study of documents stretching from the Declaration of Independence, the Constitutional Convention, the ratification debates, and other early public controversies, through court decisions, pamphlets, and manifestos, down to state papers, proclamations, official orders, laws, and constitutional amendments of the 1860s. The sheer weight of these volumes is designed to be formidable. Stephens amasses this evidence to prove a single point: that the South fought for the most fundamental American rights and freedoms. "I am content," he concludes, "notwithstanding all that is now said about 'traitors' and 'rebels,' to leave [final judgment] to the arbitrament of the intelligent, unbiased, and impartial of all times and countries. . . . By [this judgment] the Confederates, so far from being branded with the epithets of 'rebels' and 'traitors,' will be honored as 'self-sacrificing Patriots,' fighting for their Liberties throughout, and their Heroes and Martyrs in History will take places 'by the side of Washington, Hampden, and Sydney!' " (2: 667). At his most sanguine he seems to hope that his argument will stir a new call for freedom throughout the land. "Depend upon it," he warns, "there is no difference between Consolidation and Empire; no difference between Centralism and Imperialism. The consummation of either must necessarily end in the overthrow of Liberty and the establishment of Despotism" (2: 668).

At the outbreak of the American Revolution there was a rallying cry, "The cause of Boston is the cause of us all!" Stephens dares hope "that another like cry shall hereafter be raised, and go forth from hill-top to valley, from the Coast to the Lakes, from the Atlantic to the Pacific: 'The Cause of the South is the Cause of us all!' " (2: 666). But more realistically he closes with resignation and a purged conscience over a righteous cause grievously defeated:

> If the worst is to befall us; if our most serious apprehensions and gloomiest forebodings as to the future, in this respect, are to be realized; if Centralism is ultimately to prevail; if our entire system of free Institutions as established by our common ancestors is to be subverted, and an Empire is to be established in their stead; if that is to be the

last scene in the great tragic drama now being enacted: then, be assured, that we of the South will be acquitted, not only in our own consciences, but by the judgment of mankind, of all responsibility for so terrible a catastrophe, and from all the guilt of so great a crime against humanity!

(2: 669)

Stephens may seem the very type of the diehard southerner. But he cannot be easily dismissed on that account. He indulges in high-toned oratorical amplification as well as a display of unassailable erudition and weighty documents. But he is not therefore to be discounted for exaggeration; there was too much at stake for that. His attempt to make an intellectual monument to the cause of loose federalism deserves to be taken very seriously. A more pointed criticism is that he does not fully address a large body of constitutional argument, by which some founders embraced consolidation and empire as the essential grounds of American freedom. Stephens in fact ignores the forceful reasoning of his namesake, Alexander Hamilton, who was the conspicuous exponent of such ideas in the founding era.[14] This is a glaring weakness in Stephens's laborious case.

Like many other eighteenth-century political writers, Hamilton could imagine a consolidated American empire quite free from the dangers of tyranny or despotism. An "empire" in this sense was not the political arrangement for control over colonies or tributary states; it was the diversified large territory of an extended republic. It was in this sense of the term that even Thomas Jefferson, no friend of Hamilton's, could embrace an empire. "By enlarging the empire of liberty," Jefferson once wrote, "we multiply its auxiliaries, & provide new sources of renovation, should its principles, at any time, degenerate, in those portions of our country which gave them birth."[15] By word and deed, Hamilton worked to develop such an empire of liberty. Stephens acknowledges that Hamilton was the foremost "nationalist" of his time, but he tries to mine concessions from his work. He notes, for example, that at one point in the *Federalist* papers Hamilton calls the United States a "confederacy" (Stephens, 1: 45) and in another *Federalist* paper he stresses state sovereignty (Stephens, 1: 42). But Stephens ignores Hamilton's larger design in the *Federalist*, which is to justify a strong national government. In Hamilton's view, it was only through national strength that America could defend itself against foreign domination, enforce effective guarantees of liberty against local demagogues, and exploit resources for widespread prosperity. Stephens is also silent about Hamilton's successful efforts in establishing an energetic, centralized government during the Washington and Adams administrations.

In building a one-sided case, Stephens slights a debate that has always been percolating through the American Constitution. He insists that the Constitution was always federal in character, a charter of limited powers granted by sovereign states through their delegates in Philadelphia and later through the several ratifying conventions. But he thus fails to see the compromises, evasions, and manipulations of ambiguity that brought forth a nation out of a loose and ineffective wartime alliance. Hamiltonians were never completely successful in interpreting the Constitution as a blueprint for a centralized state. But then neither were their adversaries, in denying that the Constitution was more than a convenient concession of strictly limited powers. This conflict was articulate and vigorous as early as the 1790s; it shows up strikingly in the way the thinking of Hamilton and James Madison coincided and then sharply diverged between 1787, when they collaborated on the *Federalist*, and 1793, when they broke off as political enemies.[16] This dispute still figures in countless unresolved questions before American state and federal courts and legislatures.

Stephens nonetheless highlights a constitutional crisis, and thereby points in his own way to a new "epiphany of law." Whatever the Constitution may have been before 1861, it became something different thereafter. Stephens charges that the election of Lincoln was a signal that the national government intended to subjugate the South. The new administration seemed committed to undo the constitutional guarantees that southerners could hold slaves and carry them with them into federal lands to the west. Slavery was not the main cause of the war, Stephens insists; it was the issue on which the more fundamental constitutional problem came into focus. Secession, in his view, was a constitutional means by which states could protect themselves from nationalist tyranny. But the northern government insisted on retaining Fort Sumter and exercising military control over states that had legally withdrawn from the former compact. What ensued was a war of domination, won by a ruthless exercise of centralized power, and concluded by the coercions of Reconstruction. The Thirteenth and Fourteenth Amendments to the Constitution were approved by a Congress that lacked representatives from the southern states. As Stephens completed his chapters, the South was being forced to accept the latter amendment as a condition of relief from military rule.

This interpretation concerns us presently only as it bears on one point.

If Stephens is at all correct that the war in "its causes, character, causes and results" was an outbreak of imperialist tyranny, then Lincoln fills the role of arch-tyrant. He was the single person who shaped and controlled the centralized United States government from 1861 to 1865. He was the American Caesar. And by implication John Wilkes Booth was the much misunderstood American Brutus. Stephens's volumes comprise his elaborate defense and justification after the fact.

Stephens is not explicit in endorsing Booth. He does not go that far. But his extended remarks about Lincoln leave little doubt about what he felt. *A Constitutional View* is written as a series of dialogues or "colloquies" between Stephens and three fictitious northern guests at his mansion in Georgia: Judge Bynum, who represents the views of the Radical Republicans; Professor Norton, a conservative Republican; and Major Heister, a war Democrat (1: 15). Professor Norton challenges Stephens to explain how he can lay charges of despotism against the same Lincoln for whom he elsewhere professes "not only a good opinion, but even high personal regard." The professor confesses: "I always considered Mr. Lincoln . . . as eminently distinguished for his frankness, good nature and general kindness of heart." Stephens replies: "So were many men who have figured in history, and who have brought the greatest sufferings and miseries upon mankind. Danton and Robespierre, the bloodiest monsters in the form of men we read of in history, were distinguished for the same qualities" (2: 445). After justifying this last assertion, Stephens goes on to make an even sharper comparison — to Caesar.

A man may possess many amiable qualities in private life — many estimable virtues and excellencies of character, and yet in official position commit errors involving not only most unjustifiable usurpations of power, but such as rise to high crimes against society and against humanity. This, too, may be done most conscientiously and with the best intentions. This, at least, is my opinion on that subject. The history of the world abounds with apt instances for illustration. Mr. Lincoln, you say, was kind-hearted. In this, I fully agree. No man I ever knew was more so, but the same was true of Julius Caesar. All you have said of Mr. Lincoln's good qualities, and a great deal more on the same line, may be truly said of Caesar. He was certainly esteemed by many of the best men of his day for some of the highest qualities which dignify and ennoble human nature. He was a thorough scholar, a profound philosopher, an accomplished orator, and one of the most gifted, as well as polished writers of the age, in which he lived. No man ever had more devoted personal friends, and justly so, too, than he had. And yet, notwithstanding all these distinguishing, amiable and high qualities of his private character, he is by the general consent of mankind looked upon as the destroyer of the liberties of Rome!

(2: 447)

The public tyrant may be the kindliest private character. Stephens elaborates this point for over ten pages. He exonerates Lincoln of any ill-meant action. He allows that if Lincoln could have seen the carnage and devastation that he unleashed, he would have been horrified. Stephens argues that it would have been better if Lincoln had done nothing, had allowed the Union to fall to pieces and reassemble in new but wholly consensual alliances and federations, and had accepted the Confederacy's offers of compensation for public debts and joint liabilities. But Lincoln acted out of ignorance; he drove onward to catastrophe as a good man blinded by the misunderstood ideals of indissoluble union.

> In what I have said of him, I have been speaking only of his official acts—of their immediate effects and ultimate tendencies. I do not think that he intended to overthrow the Institutions of the country. I do not think he understood them or the tendencies of his acts upon them. The Union with him in sentiment, rose to the sublimity of a religious mysticism; while his ideas of its structure and formation in logic, rested upon nothing but the subtleties of a sophism!
>
> (2: 448)

This is a cold, hard, unforgiving view of Abraham Lincoln. It courteously allows much, but it frankly takes away more. Stephens nowhere expresses regret at Lincoln's death, except as an indirect cause of harsher surrender terms. His considered view is that Lincoln actively destroyed American liberties in the name of preserving the Union. Whatever his private virtues, he was a tyrant. Such a sobering charge by one symbolic figure against another can be refuted, but it cannot be denied. Stephens makes it in spite of his long and friendly acquaintance with Lincoln, because he writes on behalf of millions of Americans in the South. Lincoln certainly steeled himself to ignore and suppress a deep constitutional persuasion or tradition, which Stephens here records in grief and labors to reassert. In this view, the tragedy of Lincoln is a tragedy of American law violated, with a catastrophe that befell both the protagonist and his victims. This epiphany of law is poignant, for as Stephens wrote, the reintegration of North and

South was being forced and the ideal of the old Constitution, of states joined by ongoing choice, still seared in this writer's memory.

As we have seen, Stephens commended his vast argument to the "arbitrament of the intelligent, unbiased, and impartial of all times and countries." It is of course impossible to find pure disinterestedness in any time or place. But Stephens's charges and Lincoln's own ideals were in fact measured by another large and informed intelligence, which stood quite apart from North and South a long generation after 1865. Lord Charnwood's biography of Lincoln, published in 1916, reviews the constitutional issues of the war, if not impartially at least with sensitivity to both sides. It addresses the question of Lincoln's stature among the leaders of modern history and considers both Lincoln and Stephens in a wide view of the nineteenth century.

By the time Charnwood began writing, many of the passions of the 1860s had receded into the past. The principal statesmen and generals had grown old and died. Their memoirs and conflicting testimonies had come to light and had been assimilated and weighed by other surviving witnesses. New political problems in America had vexed a dozen presidential administrations. The country had become a continental nation of forty-eight states, with possessions in the Caribbean and the Pacific as a result of the Spanish-American War. Charnwood, meanwhile, had grown up in England, well insulated from daily reminders of Lincoln as the mythic hero of the Union or the unforgivable enemy of the South. He had studied and lectured at Oxford, served as a Liberal member of Parliament, and held local offices in Lichfield. He approached Lincoln as a leisured, highly educated foreign observer, with some direct experience of the dilemmas of public life. But he also wrote, in 1916, for a series that celebrated "Makers of the Nineteenth Century." Its general editor introduced this volume as a timely reminder of political greatness: "It is fit that the first considered attempt by an Englishman to give a picture of Lincoln, the great hero of America's struggle for the noblest cause, should come at a time when we in England are passing through as fiery a trial for a cause we feel to be as noble."[17] The task Charnwood faced was therefore to extol the public Lincoln that Stephens had attacked, to expound Lincoln's view of the Constitution, and to interpret its importance to the modern world. The result was a political biography that held the respect of both popular readers and scholars until long after Charnwood's death in 1945. Fehrenbacher could look back more than twenty years later, in the 1960s, and see Charnwood as a powerful

synthesis that led to a deeper understanding of Lincoln. "Subsequent research has diminished its value by exposing the limitations of his sources,
and yet few other books on the subject so well deserve to be labeled
'classic' " (Fehrenbacher, p. 184).

Charnwood presents Lincoln as a leader who grew to overshadow all
possible rivals because of two unique strengths. The first was his firm,
patient adherence to principles embedded in the Constitution and long
American experience. The second was his talent and desire to articulate
those principles anew at almost every important stage of his presidency.
"It was the distinction of Lincoln—a man lacking in much of the knowledge which statesmen are supposed to possess, and capable of blundering
and hesitation about details—first, that upon questions like these he was
free from ambiguity of thought or faltering of will, and further, that upon
his difficult path, amid bewildering and terrifying circumstances, he was
able to take with him the minds of very many very ordinary men"
(Charnwood, p. 121).

The principles Charnwood stresses are few and coherent. All of them
obviously clash with the conception of the Constitution developed and
defended by Stephens. Lincoln held that there could be no extension of
slavery beyond the strict limits allowed by the Constitution. There could
be no secession from the Union. Consequently, there could be no dealing
with rebel states or statesmen as if they represented any legitimate power.
And there could be no evasion of war if that was the necessary means of
preserving the United States.

To face slavery squarely Lincoln held to the familiar first axiom of the
Declaration of Independence: "that all men are created equal." This ran
directly against Stephens's firm and express belief that black people were
inherently inferior. Stephens downplays this subject in A Constitutional
View, insisting that the problems of slavery or relations between the races
were but a minor issue compared to the constitutional question that really
caused the war. But Charnwood quotes him quite otherwise in 1861, when
he defended the constitution adopted by the Confederacy:

> The new Constitution [Stephens then proclaimed] has put at rest for
> ever all the agitating questions relating to our peculiar institution,
> African slavery. This was the immediate cause of the late rupture
> and present revolution. The prevailing ideas entertained by Jefferson
> and most of the leading statesmen at the time of the old Constitution
> were that the enslavement of the African was wrong in principle
> socially, morally, and politically. Our new government is founded

upon exactly the opposite idea; its foundations are laid, its corner
stone rests, upon the great truth that the negro is not the equal of
the white man; that slavery—subordination to the white man—is
his natural and normal condition. This, our new government, is the
first in the history of the world based upon this great physical, philosophical, and moral truth. The great objects of humanity are best
attained when there is conformity to the Creator's laws and decrees.

(quoted in Charnwood, p. 178)

Stephens's modern biographer tries to extenuate this passage by explaining that it was part of a "rabble rousing" speech made soon after the
permanent Confederate constitution was adopted. But he still admits that
it was "the most notorious" passage Stephens ever delivered (Von Abele,
pp. 197-98). In a long view it was also the most suicidal. If constitutions
must rest on moral truth and divine law, then Stephens's elaborate indictment of Lincoln here falls to the dust. The racism of this passage has
been exploded by more than a century of ever more widely acknowledged
human equality. It can be understood only in view of Stephens's own
limited experience of history and southern life.

Stephens was correct, of course, in insisting that the old Constitution
had guaranteed black slavery as a peculiar institution in the South. But
Charnwood stresses that Lincoln observed that constitutional limitation to
the letter. Lincoln might appeal to the spirit of human liberation and
equality in the Declaration of Independence and make his own scholarly
arguments about the antislavery words and deeds of the founders. He did
this very conspicuously in the Cooper Union address of February 1860,
in which he forcefully insisted that slavery could and should be prohibited
in the western territories. But in this speech and elsewhere he held outrage in check against the clear constitutional guarantees of slavery in the
old South. "Wrong as we think slavery is, we can yet afford to let it alone
where it is, because that much is due to the necessity arising from its
actual presence in the nation" (*LCW*, 3: 550). As president he remained
bound by definite constitutional limits, and issued the Emancipation Proclamation only reluctantly, as a very limited war measure, after long delay,
and on the understanding that emancipation should be enlarged or established more democratically by a constitutional amendment.

Charnwood thus stresses that on this most crucial of issues Lincoln was
scrupulously observant of the Constitution; in fact he was immensely
patient to await the unfolding of its justice. Secession, rebellion, and war
faced Lincoln from the time he was elected to the presidency. Yet he held

firm against all such constitutional arguments as those developed by Stephens. Charnwood allows that he sometimes temporized, seeking more peaceful or accommodating resolutions when they seemed possible. But he did not waver about his basic conviction that he had a duty to preserve the Union by force. As the war went on for many years, Lincoln's character deepened and mellowed. He had been a laboring man, and he felt the pains and losses of common people. He saw ahead to the consequences of victory, when former enemies would have to be restored as fellow citizens. Yet he watched as millions of people lost their lives, kin, homes, or livelihood. To justify such destruction Lincoln seems to have been forced to profound religious questioning. Charnwood quotes his strange personal meditation of September 1862:

> "The will of God prevails," he wrote. "In great contests each party claims to act in accordance with the will of God. Both may be and one must be wrong. God cannot be for and against the same thing at the same time. In the present civil war it is quite possible that God's purpose is something different from the purpose of either party, and yet the human instrumentalities, working just as they do, are of the best adaptation to effect His purpose. I am almost ready to say that this is probably true, that God wills this contest, and wills that it shall not end yet. By His mere great power on the minds of the contestants, He could have either saved or destroyed the Union without a human contest. Yet the contest began, and, having begun, He could give the final victory to either side any day. Yet the contest proceeds."
>
> (Charnwood, pp. 321-22)

Yet Lincoln reached past such questioning to a persistent certainty: that the North would have to prevail if freedom were to survive in the world.

Charnwood points to this conviction as the most crucial point about Lincoln's life. "It is the central fact of this biography that no man every pondered more deeply, in his own way, or answered more firmly the question whether there was indeed an American nationality worth preserving" (p. 61). Again Charnwood sees Lincoln searching beyond the Constitution to the principle expressed in the Declaration of Independence. For him the Constitution and the union of the states were means to establish democratic government in the world and enlarge freedom for all people. To preserve the Constitution was therefore to preserve the only hope for free government in modern history.

It must never be forgotten, if we wish to enter into the spirit which sustained the North in its struggle, that loyalty for Union had a larger aspect than that of mere allegiance to a particular authority. Vividly present to the mind of some few, vaguely but honestly present to the mind of a great multitude, was the sense that even had slavery not entered into the question a larger cause than that of their recent Union was bound up with the issues of the war. The Government of the United States had been the first and most famous attempt in a great modern country to secure government by the will of the mass of the people. If in this crucial instance such a Government were seen to be intolerably weak, if it was found to be at the mercy of the first powerful minority which seized a worked-up occasion to rebel, what they had learnt to think the most hopeful agency for the uplifting of man everywhere would for ages to come have proved a failure. This feeling could not be stronger in any American than it was in Lincoln himself.

(Charnwood, pp. 182-83)

Charnwood notes that Lincoln repeated this idea often in his speeches and letters. He cites the speech at Independence Hall in 1861, when Lincoln was en route to his inauguration.

"I have never," he said, "had a feeling politically that did not spring from the sentiments embodied in the Declaration of Independence. I have often pondered over the dangers which were incurred by the men who assembled here and framed and adopted that Declaration of Independence. I have pondered over the toils that were endured by the officers and soldiers of the army who achieved that independence. I have often inquired of myself what great principle or idea it was that kept the Confederacy so long together. It was not the mere matter of separation of the colonies from the motherland, it was the sentiment in the Declaration of Independence which gave liberty, not alone to the people of this country, but I hope to the world, for all future time. It was that which gave promise that in due time the weight would be lifted from the shoulders of all men."

(Charnwood, p. 183)

Almost every American can recognize this same argument, though expressed in even more stirring phrases, in the peroration to Lincoln's message to Congress in 1862.

Fellow-citizens, *we* cannot escape history. We of this Congress and this administration, will be remembered in spite of ourselves. No personal significance, or insignificance, can spare one or another of us. The fiery trial through which we pass, will light us down, in honor or dishonor, to the latest generation. We *say* we are for the Union. The world will not forget that we say this. We know how to save the Union. The world knows we do know how to save it. We — even *we here* — hold the power, and bear the responsibility. In *giving* freedom to the *slave*, we *assure* freedom to the *free* — honorable alike in what we give, and what we preserve. We shall nobly save, or meanly lose, the last best, hope of earth.[18]

Finally, this idea has become part of the national creed in the Gettysburg Address: "Now we are engaged in a great civil war, testing whether that nation, or any nation so conceived and so dedicated, can long endure. . . . It is . . . for us to be here dedicated to the great task remaining before us . . . that government of the people, by the people, for the people, shall not perish from the earth" (*LCW*, 8: 23).

For Lincoln, then, the cause worth fighting for was the cause of liberty, just as much as it was for Stephens. It was the cause of preserving, not undermining, the Constitution, and of defending and enlarging a rare and precious political heritage. We might add that given the pressure for continental expansion, and the eventual development of continental superpowers elsewhere, Lincoln's patient tenacity in defense of human freedom was as fortunate as it was unique.[19] In any case, according to Charnwood, Lincoln was not at all blinded by zeal. Stephens had charged: "The Union with him in sentiment, rose to the subliminity of a religious mysticism." But Charnwood describes Lincoln's feelings about the Union as quite practical rather than mystical. If Lincoln was religious it was to preserve the Constitution, and even that was a subordinate means for expanding the unique American experience of liberty and human equality.

On this last point Charnwood, himself, sees limitations in Lincoln's understanding. As a good Englishman he stoutly denies that America was the only country on earth with free political institutions. He takes a very sane and distant view of the Constitution as it was originally designed.

The makers of the Constitution . . . did not, as it has often been suggested they did, create a sort of archetype and pattern for all Governments that may hereafter partake of a federal character. Nor has the curious machine which they devised — with its balanced opposition between two legislative chambers, between the whole Legislature and the independent executive power of the moment and the permanent expression of the people's will embodied in certain almost unalterable laws — worked conspicuously better than other political constitutions. The American Constitution owes its peculiarities partly to the form which the State Governments had naturally taken, and partly to sheer misunderstanding of the British Constitution, but much more to the want at the time of any strong sense of national unity and to the existence of a good deal of dislike to all government whatsoever.

(Charnwood, pp. 22-23)

He also charges that the practical operations of the Constitution had become stagnant by the time of Andrew Jackson.

There were now few genuine issues in politics. Compromise on vital questions was understood to be the highest statesmanship. The Constitution itself, with its curious system of checks and balances, rendered it difficult to bring anything to pass. Added to this was a party system with obvious natural weaknesses, infected from the first with a dangerous malady [i.e., the spoils system]. The political life, which lay on the surface of the national life of America, thus began to assume an air of futility, and, it must be added, of squalor.

(p. 50)

Charnwood even concedes that Lincoln's most celebrated single accomplishment—the emancipation of the slaves—was possible only because an extraordinary constitutional crisis briefly placed the necessary power and opportunity in his hands alone (p. 312).

Lincoln nevertheless served worthwhile principles, for both America and the world; he refrained from acting beyond clear constitutional limits; and he rightly understood that the Constitution embodied ideals of permanent value. Charnwood finally celebrates his courage and wisdom in managing very crude and delicate instruments of democracy. "The fittest machinery for popular government, the machinery through which the real judgment of the people will prevail, can only by degrees and after many failures be devised. Popular government was then young, and it is young still" (p. 50).

Moreover, the strength of his principles was only one side of Lincoln's greatness. He could also give life to those principles; raise them above the level of dry, legalistic, constitutional correctness; and inspire multitudes to surmount disaster for their sake. This was certainly not the gift of Stephens or many other American statesmen of that time. In part it was a gift of sheer political acumen. "To the end he showed no intuitive comprehension of individual men. His sincere friendly intention, the unanswerable force of an argument, the convincing analogy veiled in an unseemly story, must take their chance of suiting the particular taste of Senator Sherman or

General McClellan; but any question of managing men in the mass . . . involved an element of subtle and long-sighted calculation which was vastly congenial to him" (p. 73). In larger part it was a habit of long experience in appealing to common people.

Charnwood notes that Lincoln was not only awkwardly built but positively ungainly. He also had a jarring, high-pitched voice. Yet he could project an irresistible appeal. In the political conditions of western America he could not have survived otherwise. "Lincoln's wisdom had to utter itself in a voice that would reach the outskirts of a large and sometimes excited crowd in the open air" (p. 132). Of course it had to reach further as well: to the councils of party officials, for example, or the quiet desks of careful, critical readers. But Lincoln's deepest appeal was a simple, forthright commonness. He could show the same penetrating consideration to a black intellectual like Frederick Douglass or an ambitious general like Joseph Hooker, to a weak soldier boy or a seedy office-seeker, to a radical abolitionist or an old colleague with southern sympathies. He genuinely, directly paid attention to every kind of human being. "Except when his indignation was kindled, he was abnormally reluctant to say 'no,' — he once shuddered to think what would have happened to him if he had been a woman, but was consoled by the thought that his ugliness would have been a shield" (p. 234).

His principles and his oratory were thus of a piece. And, we might add, they were of a piece with his era. They correspond with the old-fashioned theater of declamatory tragedy, addressed to an eager audience made up of people of all conditions. If Lincoln worked to free the slaves, it was after he had worked to free himself from the shackles of poverty and ignorance. If he believed that America was the last best hope of earth, it was because it had fulfilled the most ambitious hopes of the disadvantaged man he had been. If he continued to crack simple or unseemly jokes in the midst of cabinet meetings over which he held intellectual mastery, it was because he never lost touch with his native earth. In Charnwood's estimation he was a larger human being than any of his contemporaries; this biography repeatedly measures other statesmen against Lincoln and finds them smaller, especially if they failed to perceive his complexity.

The implication is plain: Lincoln drew into his own character the essential truths of American experience and so attained a larger vision of his country and its ideals than anyone else ever has. With his gifts of oratory he became the preeminent historian of the Civil War, rightly interpreting its events as they unfolded. What is more, he impressed that interpretation upon his generation in language simple, moving, and memorable: he became the supreme poet of American democracy. His actions as president can be read properly only in his own language about them, and his writings can be understood properly only in relation to his consistent acts of statesmanship. It is in the character of Lincoln that we find the epiphany of law — both American justice and the modern understanding of individual human worth.

From our perspective in the late twentieth century, Charnwood's idealism may now look dated in its turn. This is the voice of privileged nineteenth-century British liberalism. And if it finds its counterpart in Lincoln, it does so with evident distortions and an edge of strain. "Those who read Lincoln's important letters and speeches," Charnwood writes, "see in him at once a great gentleman" (p. 404). But Charnwood has to devote many long passages to justifying and defending that claim with respect to the living man. The phenomenon of Lincoln continues to astonish the civilized British eye. How could "this specially grotesque specimen of the wild West" (p. 156), nurtured among "crude people with a narrow horizon" (p. 62), have become a gentleman? "Wife and tailor combined could not, with any amount of money, have dressed him well" (p. 86). To his contemporaries he remained a crude-looking, strange-acting puzzle. It is not altogether surprising that he surpassed most other American politicians of his time; the political society of Washington in 1864 "was on the average as poor in brain and heart as the court of the most decadent European monarchy" (p. 415). But Charnwood develops the character of Lincoln as a unique blend of wisdom, simplicity, cunning, and courage — a rare human figure in the history of the world. He cannot altogether discount the idea that it was the miraculous hand of Providence that brought Lincoln to power at the time of his country's greatest need (p. 167). We may well wonder if Charnwood is not seeing Lincoln with the enthusiasm of the converted, or finding in this one exceptional man some justification for the emergence of America as a modern world power. And we should properly question whether one great man could rightly symbolize the complex America of the modern age, or even of the 1860s.

These estimates of character by Stephens and Charnwood do not so much answer each other as reveal that Lincoln can seem tragic in many ways, and can be projected as tragic from many motives. Taken together, these two observers bring out the limitations of using the term tragedy to give shape to the Lincoln myth.

To Stephens, Lincoln was the perpetrator of a grievous cosmic irony.

Lincoln meant well personally but he stumbled into a public career that destroyed the consensual foundation of American liberty. "I do not think that he intended to overthrow the Institutions of the country. I do not think he understood them or the tendencies of his acts upon them." The issue of slavery gave the Republicans in the North a pretext for exercising consolidated national power. Lincoln as their leader was a kind and cordial man, but he became the wielder of destruction. He became a Caesar. And of course he died a Caesar's death.

To Charnwood the tragedy is much richer, for the irony yields powerful moments of recognition. Lincoln was not blind but gifted with a deep understanding of a libertarian tradition. He sought public notice out of a vigorous public spirit. When he came into power he managed it prudently and humbly. The inexorable logic of secession, armed conflict, and protracted war drove him through a fiery trial of grief and spiritual questioning. But he remained steadfast to his principles and deepened in his wisdom. He knowingly approved acts that devastated whole regions and ultimately provoked his own death. But his last speeches witness his rise to the tragic hero's awesome comprehension of his place in the universe.

To all other observers Lincoln has had to remain fixed in some such memorable pattern. The stubborn facts of his presidency can hardly be framed except by some pattern of tragedy. Unlike any other president, Lincoln served an entire term of office that was devoted to one great issue. His presidency was shaped like a tragedy, with a clearly marked unity of action. His election was the immediate cause of secession. Every day of his administration was filled with measures for countering secession. His death directly followed the capitulation of the secessionist states. His time as leader was therefore exactly congruous with the period of the Civil War. The collective griefs of that conflict found their final full expression in public grief over his violent death. In the midst of the war he achieved what the Declaration of Independence seemed to require but the Constitution could not effect; with a stroke of the pen, he freed the slaves. Yet he paid for that act with his life.

And his final weeks comprised a rapid sequence of dramatic turns. His second inauguration (March 4) seemed to symbolize a triumph of democracy — free elections in wartime, reaffirming his policies and constitutional legitimacy. Within weeks (April 9) Lee surrendered and received generous terms from Grant, harbingers of a peaceful reunion of North and South. Then within a few days (April 14) Booth fired his single shot. The war ended with the first violent overthrow of a president, a shock as severe as the opening fire on Fort Sumter just four years earlier. Lincoln's end still handily symbolizes the complicated legal, political, and moral dilemmas of his time. His personal death continues to stand for the breakdown of the nation. It serves as a focus for feeling in place of deliberate political thought. And it eases the catastrophe of a constitution torn apart and never quite restored, by highlighting the solace of Lincoln's words, which have endured to a life beyond sordid violence.

But if this is history Stephens may help us remember that tragedy is a very frightening pattern for it. Tragedy, after all, depends on the concentration of power as well as wisdom in one person. And concentrated power is antithetical to either popular government or constitutional restraint. "Power generally seems to change and transform the characters of those invested with it," Stephens writes at the end of his paragraph about Lincoln and his blind devotion to the Union. "Hence, the great necessity for 'those chains' in the Constitution, to bind all Rulers and men in authority, spoken of by Mr. Jefferson" (Stephens, 2: 448). To thoughtful libertarians, tragedy must always be suspect. It cannot justify an imperial leader, however personally worthy.

Likewise Charnwood may help us remember that tragedy provides a seductive pattern for political biography. All errors, frailties, and disadvantages can seem minor or even fortuitous as they take their place in a course toward a brilliant and moving conclusion. A victory of sheer might can seem a victory of high principle. One's sympathies for a doomed leader can becloud a tangle of public issues, leaving the impression that only his way could lead to justice. Achievements of eloquence can be confused with achievements of enduring statesmanship, which are not at all the same. Charnwood certainly catches Stephens out by revealing how he frankly avowed slavery as the foundation of the Confederacy. But Charnwood in turn makes an argument with a gaping hole in it. If slavery could be ended, as it proved, only by force; if the Constitution could be preserved only by a civil war; and if Lincoln was indeed the unique wise man who could control and exercise such power—then where in fact was the widespread, active, diffuse "machinery for popular government" that was the soul of American democracy? Where, that is, besides in Lincoln's unique reading of the will of "our fathers"? If Lincoln's death marked the collapse of his ideals as a program for practical action, and the opening of bitter Reconstruction and a century and more of racial agony, then how could he not have been far afield from the abiding political sentiments of his living fellow Americans? He may have been wiser and more just,

but if he was tragic he was alone. "This man had stood alone in the dark,"
Charnwood writes. "He had done justice; he had loved mercy; he had
walked humbly with his God" (p. 438). If he was so alone, he was out
of touch with the vital democracy he kept claiming to defend, though
he spoke in its voice and in its native idiom.

"In no other contest in history," Charnwood writes, "are those elements
in human affairs on which tragic dramatists are prone to dwell so clearly
marked as in the American Civil War" (p. 180). This is a patent exaggeration, especially from a man who doubtless knew the accounts of Troy
in the original Greek. But we all know what Charnwood means. And he
comes closer to the truth in binding that tragic understanding to Lincoln's
eloquence. In discussing the Second Inaugural Address he notes its "language of intense religious feeling" as the final expression for a fully
enlightened soul. "Here is one of the few speeches ever delivered by a
great man at the crisis of his fate on the sort of occasion which a tragedian
telling his story would have devised for him" (p. 438). No one, I think,
cares to deny the power that inspires such a judgment.

> With malice toward none; with charity for all; with firmness in the
> right, as God gives us to see the right, let us strive on to finish the
> work we are in; to bind up the nation's wounds; to care for him who
> shall have borne the battle, and for his widow, and his orphan — to
> do all which may achieve a just, and lasting peace, among ourselves,
> and with all nations.
>
> (*LCW*, VII, 333)

But the power of these words derives from their hope, for their promises
still unfulfilled. Lincoln seems to see all, if we regard him as "a great man
at the crisis of his fate." But what he sees here has not come to be. Nor
could it have, if he had lived. Whether it was a personal, a national, or
a prophetic modern vision, Lincoln as tragic hero could give us only a
flickering epiphany. That is all any tragic hero can do. He dies, while the
laws that showed through him remain eternal and mysterious.

6

John Wilkes Booth
as Brutus

*T*HE ASSASSINATION of Lincoln
may seem to echo and revitalize many lines of an ancient legend. Like
Julius Caesar, Lincoln died at a height of personal and national fortune.
And John Wilkes Booth explicitly thought of himself as a Brutus defeating
a tyrant. But in the particulars of its place, time, and performance, Booth's
act was a shabby travesty of the ancient fall of the emperor.

In the first place, nineteenth-century Washington was a setting hardly
comparable to the grandeur that was Rome. It was still an out-of-the-way
small city, still raw in a country less than a century old; a city, too, crowded
and dislocated by an influx of soldiers, officials, and office-seekers during
the war. It did have a Capitol Hill with an imposing classical Capitol,
whose new dome had at last been completed, with great and pompous
celebration, in 1863. And the Capitol looked out to the west over a creek
that had been dubbed the Tiber. But such pretensions had long been
ridiculed in America. Even in Jefferson's time the Irish poet Thomas
Moore had written perceptive neoclassical couplets from the city of
Washington:

> 'Tis evening now; beneath the western star
> Soft sighs the lover through his sweet segar,

And fills the ears of some consenting she
With puffs and vows, with smoke and constancy.
The patriot, fresh from Freedom's councils come,
Now pleas'd retires to lash his slaves at home. . . .
    In fancy now, beneath the twilight gloom
Come, let me lead thee o'er this "second Rome!"
Where tribunes rule, where dusky Davi bow,
And what was Goose-Creek once is Tiber now:—
This embryo capital, where Fancy sees
Squares in morasses, obelisks in trees;
Which second-sighted seers, ev'n now, adorn
With shrines unbuilt and heroes yet unborn.[1]

Countless visitors recorded that Washington did not change much in the first half of the century. In the 1860s it was surrounded by forts and military works and invaded by thousands of soldiers, sailors, clerks, politicians, and opportunists. But it remained a place of "shrines unbuilt." The ugly stump of the Washington Monument was still a national disgrace on the Mall, near mud flats where army cattle grazed beside an open sewage canal. Well-known photographs show Ford's Theatre crowded among dull buildings on one of the city's notorious unpaved streets. In the spring such thoroughfares became sluices of liquid mud. "The city of Washington, the capital of the nation, is probably the dirtiest and most ill-kept borough in the United States." So wrote a newspaper correspondent in late March 1863.

It is impossible to describe the truly fearful condition of the streets; they are seas or canals of liquid mud, varying in depth from one to three feet, and possessing as geographical features, conglomerations of garbage, refuse and trash. . . . At some points, where a street has a sloping intersection with another, I have seen a torrent of thick, yellow mud flowing in unruffled smoothness over the concealed crossing, bearing on its placid surface the unconsidered trifles which have been swept out of saloons, shops and houses. Through such masses as this labor the unfortunate animals which are condemned to drudge their miserable life in such a wretched vocation as falls to the lot of a Government-contract horse.[2]

It was past or over such muck that Lincoln's body was carried back to the Executive Mansion on the rainy morning of April 15.

Nor was April 14 anything like the old Ides of March, except that both were midmonth days of spring. For Caesar the Ides was a date for assuming new powers before conducting new wars. Lincoln's date was apparently a moment for relaxation when victory was at hand. If the date was momentous it augured poorly for Booth. His stupidest blunder may have been timing his attack on Good Friday at the end of the war. The moment could not have been better calculated for rendering Lincoln the martyr saint of the Union, and for raising new vows of vengeance against the South, from even the most devout Christian spirit.

But Booth and his accomplices were hardly to be compared to a band of honorable, intelligent Roman senators. They were boardinghouse misfits who could not have sustained or understood an intricate political debate. They fell apart even as a gang of murderers: one shirking his assignment to kill the vice president; another brutally but not mortally gashing the secretary of state, once he found him defenseless in his bed. None of them except Booth had any prior claim to public attention. And Booth was left, or chose, to act alone by stealth. Cassius and Brutus had faced Caesar openly as they stabbed him in plain view of the Roman senate. Booth slipped up into a hidden nook, drew out a concealed pistol, and fired from behind into Lincoln's unsuspecting brain.

Such was the murder of Lincoln, and its aftermath was just as squalid. Lincoln languished overnight in a house across from the theater, his long body laid diagonally across the bed of a crowded little room. Booth fled into the night and slowly made his way to Virginia. Instead of a hero's welcome or a sudden uprising of support he found a few cautious people willing to hide him and a partner and move them along. Within two weeks federal officers tracked him to a barn near Port Royal. The barn was set afire before dawn, and Booth stumbled out with a bullet wound through the vertebrae of his neck. An erratic, self-castrated sergeant named "Boston" Corbett claimed to have shot at him through the slats of the burning barn when Booth raised his own weapons. Though Corbett's claim was long denied, no one could absolutely prove him wrong. After Booth died on the farmhouse porch, his body was carried back to Washington and ignominiously dumped under the floor of a military prison. His fellow conspirators were arrested and hastily tried by a military court; four were hanged and buried just outside the building where Booth still lay.

It takes an effort of imagination to make details like these resemble the classic outlines of Brutus against Caesar, especially as these characters had been refined by two centuries of Shakespearean acting. Of course it takes an effort of imagination to make any murder resemble a work of art. But if Booth was a Brutus, the press soon reminded the world that he was also a romantic matinee idol, "a Confederate doing duty on his own responsibility," a speculator in oil fields, a spoiled mama's boy, and finally the villain in a Wild West melodrama—complete with flagrant womanizing, hard drinking, gunshots, reward posters, chase, and showdown. In fact Booth lived out all these roles and more. A reader tracking him must learn to look for a chameleon, an actor of many roles, a figure of thin veneer upon veneer. If he is a Brutus, he is one whose toga keeps slipping, who has and then doesn't have a thick black mustache on his marble bust, who carries a pistol (and then a carbine and a pair of crutches) along with the bloody dagger he brandished on stage.

When the first shock had passed and people could begin to find terms for the assassination, it was inevitable that Brutus and Caesar should be mentioned. Lincoln was the first American president to be assassinated; he had just been the most powerful of all presidents; the crime could seem as enormous as any in history. To those who sympathized with Booth, it could seem almost as noble. But the Roman names often appear in contexts that point out the strain of such a comparison.

There was a widely circulated poem about Booth, supposed to have been written by a Texas general, Alexander W. Terrell. When set to music by E. B. Armand it was published as "Our Brutus"—and it was still being quoted in southern lecture halls in the 1890s.[3] But the title page of the song carries an engraving of Booth not as a noble Roman but as a soft-eyed gentleman from a mid-nineteenth-century drawing room. And the main burden of the song has little to do with Rome. It is that a hero so large deserves burial in the sea. The words were preserved in Asia Booth Clarke's memorial album for her brother. They show that (among other faults) the writer had a very muddled sense of history concerning Brutus and the Roman emperors:

> He has died for the weal of a world 'neath the heel
> Of too many a merciless Nero—
>   But while there is steel
>   Every tyrant shall feel
> That God's justice but waits for its hero.

The words "our Brutus" occur only in the final stanza:

> Give him a sepulchre broad as the sweep
> Of the tidal wave's measureless motion,
>   Lay our Brutus to sleep
>   In the arms of the deep,
> Since his life was as free as the ocean.[4]

There was a more pointed comparison in the 1865 diary of Charles Mason, an Iowa politician who witnessed Lincoln's elaborate funeral in Washington. The funeral was arranged at great public expense. In the end it involved the procession of a special train back through almost all the major cities of the North. City after city vied to present the most elaborate floral, oratorical, and architectural displays of public grief; it took until May 3 before Lincoln's body at last reached Springfield, Illinois. During all this time the corpse was kept prepared for public display by embalmers who traveled with it. No photographs were allowed, but hundreds of thousands of viewers were meant to see Lincoln's eyes and cheeks still discolored from the effects of Booth's bullet. Edwin Stanton, the secretary of war, explicitly prohibited any attempt by the undertakers to restore Lincoln's face. He wanted the people to see a martyr still bearing the marks of his suffering.[5] Charles Mason witnessed the early stages of these funeral plans, and they reminded him of the "crafty skill of Mark Anthony in displaying to the Roman people the bloody mantle of Caesar." Mason accurately saw that the radical Republicans intended "to make all the political capital possible out of this murder. They wish to strengthen their own hands and brutalize the hearts of the northern people till there shall be a general concurrence in all the measures of confiscation and exter- mination which they desire and contemplate."[6] The point of the allusion here, of course, is not that Booth was a Brutus. It is rather that the northern Republicans were unwittingly making him one. By reenacting the funeral of Caesar and consolidating power over the corpse of Lincoln, they were creating the tyranny Booth had claimed to oppose.

Booth himself carried a pocket notebook as he fled from Washington, and in it he recorded his own comparison to Brutus. One entry is backdated to "April 13 — 14 Friday the Ides'"[7] and it describes his motives and actions on the night of the assassination. Another entry, dated April 21, mentions Brutus explicitly in a passage of immense self-pity and heroic posturing:

> After being hunted like a dog through swamps, woods, and last night being chased by gun-boats till I was forced to return wet cold and starving, with every man's hand against me, I am here in despair. And why? For doing what Brutus was honored for. What made Tell a Hero. And yet I for striking down a greater tyrant than they ever knew am looked upon as a common cutthroat. My action was purer than either of theirs. One hoped to be great himself. The other had not only his country's but his own wrongs to avenge. I hoped for no gain. I knew no private wrong. I struck for my country and that

alone. A country groaned beneath this tyranny and prayed for this
end, and yet now behold the cold hand they extend to me.

Thus does Booth make Brutus his inferior. Like William Tell, Brutus had
ulterior motives for what he did. Booth had none. He struck "for my
county and that alone." Here he claims to be Brutus and at the same time
scorns the comparison.

What all the evidence seems to show is that as a Brutus, John Wilkes
Booth was a study in bathos, a man too young, self-centered, flashy, clumsy,
and mindless to bear the weight of a classical hero for long. He did kill
a great man at the height of power, in the capital city of a vast country;
he did elicit some sympathy for bringing down a tyrant. But these facts
have never been enough to offset Booth's evident theatrical vulgarity and
Lincoln's human depth.

Yet from another perspective Booth remains a compelling figure. He
remains memorable long after many other shabby assassins have been
forgotten. He was able, after all, to assault Lincoln in a place that was in
a way his own domain. He was able to improvise and carry out one of
the most striking performances in the history of the American theater.

This is the most significant parallel to be drawn between Booth and
Brutus: both were able instantaneously to both complete and vividly dramatize their political murders. The Roman conspirators succeeded in drawing Caesar into their special chamber, the meeting place of the senate, and
they stabbed him there in a concerted order until he fell at the base of
Pompey's statue. After months of feckless plotting to abduct Lincoln, Booth
suddenly found a way open to kill him instead. He was given the occasion
to trap the president in a box directly over a well-lit stage, and he acted
quickly to make the most of it.

April 14 saw a rapid sequence of changes in plan, which gave several
different meanings to the performance scheduled that night at Ford's
Theatre. In retrospect it seems that Booth was the one person who could
comprehend them all and drive them to a single coherent purpose.

What was originally scheduled was a well-worn if not threadbare comedy
about British and American manners, Our American Cousin by Tom
Taylor. (This was the same playwright who had once collaborated on a
stage version of Uncle Tom's Cabin, and who in 1865 wrote a sudden ode
of remorse in Punch for satires against Lincoln during his lifetime.)[8] The
play was written in England in 1850 but was first produced in 1858 in
America. The plot traces the arrival in England of Asa Trenchard, a rough-
hewn but lovable Vermont Yankee. He sees through the sham of his British

relatives, their servants, and their toadies, and he generously saves their fortunes for them. The play is a farce, sheer entertainment, but with a strong undercurrent of pride in American ways. Its first production company — Joseph Jefferson, Laura Keene, and Edward A. Sothern — had made it over into a hit full of famous stage business, which brought the two male actors sudden stardom. Sothern rigged himself up as a preposterous Lord Dundreary, with dyed hair, a claret-colored frock coat, a lisp, a stutter, an ever-impending sneeze, and a jiggling shuffle. Jefferson became Asa Trenchard: "I'm a rough sort of customer, and don't know much about the ways of great folks, I've got a cool head, a stout arm, and a willing heart, and I think I can help you just as one cousin ought to help another."[9] Both actors toured in these roles for years.

Much of the play consists of jokes and routines certain to fill the house with loud laughter. In act 3, scene 2, a scheming Mrs. Mountchessington forces her daughter away from Asa Trenchard once she learns he has given away his inheritance. According to Harry Hawk, the actor who played Trenchard at this performance, this was the point at which the murder occurred. "She turned haughtily and made her exit on the left," Hawk recalls, "leaving me alone and looking after her." At this moment Trenchard's lines read: "Don't know the manners of good society, eh? Well, I guess I know enough to turn you inside out, old gal — you sockdologizing old man-trap." Hawk reports: "I was looking up at the President's box as I repeated the lines, and the words barely left my lips, and the shouts of laughter were ringing, when the shot sounded through the house."[10] Booth may well have calculated his moves so that he fired when the president was intent on the play and the house was full of noise from these comic lines. He could have known the play well enough to strike at just this point; he had performed in it in a run of a dozen nights in Richmond in 1859. "Sockdologer" is a slang term for a heavy, decisive blow (a combination of "sock" and "doxology"); and for Booth this performance was a very fortuitous "man-trap." In any case, he caught Lincoln while he was enjoying the kind of humor he had long relished: quips in American dialect from good-hearted common people who see the world better than their pretentious social superiors.

Laura Keene was featured that night as Flora Trenchard, the winning young English cousin. As the playbills indicated, she had played the role over a thousand times already. In fact she owned the script. This was her final night in Washington — a benefit; so, apart from seeing a comic hit, many in the audience would have been attracted by this famous star playing one of her most celebrated characters. Laura Keene, like many others in Ford's Theatre, was well acquainted with the Booths. It was she who had set up Edwin to tour Australia from San Francisco when he was just beginning his career in the 1850s, and young John Wilkes had started his career in what was called Laura Keene's Theatre in Baltimore in 1855.[11] (In 1865 she was nearly forty—a bit old perhaps for an alluring kissing cousin in anything but a play like this one, but still a popular attraction.) As a star himself, Booth had free access to all parts of Ford's Theatre; he had acted there as recently as March 18. As an old acquaintance he could slip unobtrusively here and there without question from Keene or any of the other theater people. What was billed was a lighthearted comedy with a popular actress, a sheer escape from the worries of the capital at war's end. Why should anyone notice an idle actor lurking backstage or in the lobby or gallery?

The tone of the performance was changed a little by the news that the president would attend. The original arrangement was for the Lincolns and the Grants to share a box over the stage. Workmen were assigned to remove a partition between two boxes, arrange the furniture, and decorate the front of the enlarged "state box" with flags and a portrait of George Washington. New handbills were printed, announcing a patriotic song, "Honor to Our Soldiers," to be sung by the cast.

Many people frowned at the thought of the theater on Good Friday, especially for a frivolous farce while the war was still going on. "It was the moan of the religious people, the one throb of anguish to hero worshipers, that the President had not gone first to a place of worship, or [had not] remained at home on this jubilant occasion. It desecrated his idea to have his end come in a devil's den—a theater—in fact." So wrote the Booths's sister Asia, familiar with what people thought of the theater, and with her own layers of bitterness. "That fatal visit to the theater had no pity in it; it was jubilation over fields of unburied dead, over miles of desolated homes" (UB, p. 139). In retrospect, there were plenty of hints and warnings Lincoln should have heeded, more than reached Caesar on his way to the senate. But on April 14 he went to the theater anyhow. This was a special Good Friday. The war seemed virtually finished; the city of Washington was ready to relax. And there was Mrs. Lincoln to consider. The newspaper correspondent Noah Brooks recorded seeing the president that afternoon and being told that the Lincolns had almost invited him to join their party. Late in the day the president "had felt inclined to give up the whole thing," but the announcements were already in the newspapers and "Mrs. Lincoln had rather insisted that they ought to go, in order that the expectant public should not be wholly disappointed" (Brooks, pp. 213-14).

By early evening, then, theatergoers were preparing for an evening of comedy enhanced by patriotism. The play was a celebration of America. It would star a popular actress who had made America her home. There would be a song for the soldiers who had served in the war just ending. And Grant the hero and Lincoln the president would sit in the state box just above the stage.

But by this time the Grants had broken off their part of the engagement and left Washington by train to see their children at a school in New Jersey. This explanation was probably a polite evasion. Mrs. Grant heartily disliked Mrs. Lincoln and refused to accompany her husband, and Edwin Stanton also urged Grant not to go, so that the president might be discouraged from attending and exposing himself to danger at the theater.[12] To replace the Grants, Mrs. Lincoln invited a younger couple, Major Henry R. Rathbone and his fiancée Clara Harris. (She was the daughter of Senator Ira T. Harris of New York, who was also Rathbone's stepfather.) This arrangement set up an entirely different tableau in the state box. Instead of the president and the hero who had accepted Lee's surrender, the audience was to welcome two prominent couples. Booth could see that he had lost his chance to kill two giants at once, but he might also face less danger in personal combat with a slight man like Major Rathbone.

From this point on, the events of the evening are obscured by the sheer multitude of details remembered by dozens of witnesses. What occurred was stunning and, as commonly happens, many people who saw or took part in it were shocked into temporary amnesia followed by fanciful reconstruction. Later questions provoked further distorted and conflicting answers. Exactly when the Lincoln party arrived at the theater; when, how, and where Booth stood, leapt, and moved across the stage; what in fact he shouted — these are among the questions that have received far too many authentic answers.

But everyone agrees about the rough architectural plan of Ford's Theatre, and the fact that Lincoln was shot there in a special box. This box could be perceived in many ways, and what happened within it was therefore not simple. The assassination, as a publicly witnessed event, was a combination of perceptions and feelings about that box and its relation to the stage, the audience, and the world.

From the outside the box was a symbol of patriotism and legitimate authority. It was decorated with flags and the picture of Washington. It was set up so that Lincoln would be framed by these decorations while the company on stage sang a patriotic song and the audience signaled its approval. On this particular occasion no other boxes were occupied, though the theater was crowded. The state box was set off as unique. It was also placed in a privileged relation to the stage, directly even with it (forward of the other seats on the main floor or in the gallery) and several feet above it. The occupants could look down at actors very close to them, and also see into the secrets of the wings. Quite evidently, this performance depended on the presence of the state box to complete the celebration of a patriotic evening (and legitimate a packed house on a Good Friday). The delayed arrival of the Lincoln party created a tension, relieved by a sudden break in the action on stage, the orchestra's playing "Hail to the Chief," and the president's standing at the front of the box to acknowledge the welcome.

During the performance that followed, some people in the audience could look up to the box hoping to catch a glimpse of the people there, although they were obscured from most viewers. There were also one or two touches in the play that should have drawn the whole house into good shared laughter. In the dairy scene, for example, the ever-frail Georgina complains that she can no longer sit outdoors. She appeals to Dundreary: "If you please, ask the dairy maid to let me have a seat in the dairy. I'm afraid of the draft here." Dundreary has a ready reply:

> Oh, you want to get out of the draft, do you? Well, you're not the only one that wants to escape the draft.

But for this performance the line was changed:

> You are mistaken. The draft has already been stopped by order of the President!

To which there was laughter followed by solid applause (Bryan, p. 173). A few moments later, Asa catches a peep of the same frail Georgina, now taking a bit of refreshment in the cottage.

> I wonder how that sick gal is getting along. Wal, darn me, if the dying swallow ain't pitching into ham and eggs and homemade bread, wal, she's walking into the fodder like a farmer arter a day's work rail splitting.
>
> (Taylor, p. 211)

Any comic worth his salt should have paused and devised some stage business at this point to get a laugh right under the nose of the most celebrated rail-splitter ever known.

On the inside, the box was not an official place at all, but a comfortable domestic chamber. Ford's Theatre had been rebuilt in 1863, and this box in particular had been prepared and furnished to make its occupants feel at ease. The arrival of the two couples, the long-married Lincolns and the hopeful younger pair, nicely matched these preparations. After careful study George S. Bryan described the double box as a small irregular room with a frontage (toward the stage) "of between ten and twelve feet. A pillar rising from the balustrade divided the face of the box into two lofty arches from which hung draperies of buff satin and curtains of Nottingham lace. The walls were covered with a dark, figured paper; the floor was laid with Turkey carpet. In front was suspended what one newspaper styled 'a chaste chandelier' " (Bryan, p. 169). Within this little room the younger couple were seated on a sofa against the far wall, with Clara Harris closest to the stage. The president sat in a handsome rocking chair brought down for him from Harry Ford's own room in an adjacent building. Mary Lincoln sat to his right in an armchair. Here, in other words, were two couples in well-upholstered seclusion, settled for an evening of special hospitality and amusement, almost nestled in a place purposely cut off from the cares of state and the cautions of war.

But Booth had a different idea. To him the box offered striking opportunities, in many senses of the term. It was a focal point, a place where he could make a dramatic gesture: a state box framing Lincoln as president, where his end would be witnessed by hundreds of assembled spectators. It was also a hidden, confined space. Behind the boxes was a small vestibule where Booth could prepare his weapon out of sight of anyone and move with deliberate suddenness to his attack. And it was a box just a leap away from the stage, a place adjacent to Booth's own realm where he could be recognized for his deed before making a swift and effective escape.

Booth's shot may have seemed (and may still seem) unspeakably hideous just because his use of the box perverted what everyone else understood about it. His act suddenly changed a house united in good feeling to a place chaotic with shock, grief, fear, anger, and guilt. It left a sense of violated space. Booth had easily broken into, then almost playfully vaulted out of what was ostentatiously set up as a raised national shrine. He had shot a defenseless Lincoln and stabbed Major Rathbone, and in the act he had brought war right into a cosy little parlor, threatening women in evening clothes and shedding blood before their eyes. The play that night had reached out across the footlights to welcome Lincoln into its particular kind of comedy. For an actor then to leap upon the stage with Lincoln's blood on his hands was an outrage against the theater, against hospitality, against every expected decency.

Booth had been planning it all day, if not all week. For months he had been plotting to abduct Lincoln and carry him south as a hostage so that the North would again release captive Confederate soldiers. After missing his chance on a couple of occasions, Booth had abandoned this plan. But as the war drew to an end, his anger toward Lincoln seems to have grown more intense. Lincoln had entered Richmond personally just after the Confederate government had fled on April 4. On April 11, back in Washington, he made a brief speech at the White House, in favor of suffrage for literate black men. Witnesses later recorded angry outbursts by Booth over both these events.[13] But the idea of murdering Lincoln probably came to him suddenly, when he heard on the morning of the fourteenth that Lincoln and Grant would be in the state box that night. For the rest of the day he was busy with preparations. He hired a horse for his escape. He may have sent Mrs. Surratt (later hanged as his accomplice) into southern Maryland to scout his route and to carry some of his effects ahead for him. He called together the men he assigned to attack the vice president and secretary of state. He tried to call on the vice president himself (whom he had met earlier in Nashville), perhaps to beg the favor of a pass through the guarded exits from Washington. In the street he met John Matthews, an actor who was to perform that night in *Our American Cousin*. Booth gave Matthews a "paper sealed and stamped" and asked him to deliver it personally the next morning at the office of the *National Intelligencer*.[14] It also seems that he went into the theater and made his way to the state box at some unguarded moment in order to tamper with its doors, boring a peephole in one so that he could see the president from the passageway behind the box, and fixing a way to brace a wooden rod from within, so that no one could easily enter the box area after him (Kimmel, p. 218).

The long or short background to the assassination then gave way to its execution. Once the performance had begun and the Lincolns were in their seats, Booth began to take possession of Ford's Theatre. There is no better way to put it. More than any other person that night he explored the whole building, looping his way from the alley in back to the street in front, from the basement to the gallery, circling the state box before he struck. He arrived at the rear and got a stagehand to come out and hold the reins of his horse. Then, because the dairy scene was still running and taking up the full depth of the stage, he went down under the stage and across to a side exit, through an alley, and into Taltavull's saloon where he ordered a whiskey. Later, after an intermission in the play, Booth was seen in the theater lobby and kidding at the box office with that night's manager, Harry Ford. As the next scene came on, he went up the stairs to the gallery or dress circle and made his way behind the back row of seats across the theater and down to the doorway to the boxes. There was no guard posted in the vestibule. The officer assigned to duty there had taken a seat in the audience, as had the president's footman. By some pretext or other (accounts vary) Booth overcame a mere verbal challenge from the footman and went through the forbidden door.

From his easy, unhampered movement through the theater, it is evident that Booth might have taken a shot at Lincoln without getting into the state box. He might have fired up from the wings, or slipped down to the front of the orchestra section. With the advantage of surprise, it is even conceivable that he could have rushed onto the dairy scene of this silly comedy and paused to take careful aim with a long rifle. (Asa Trenchard appears in Act 2 in preposterous archery dress, and is chided for not bringing his costume for hunting buffalo.) But Booth was moving through more than space. He was moving through many roles. He was a backstage member of the theater company, then a drinking companion in the saloon next door, then a teasing acquaintance of the manager and ticket taker, then a quiet spectator in the gallery, then a dark man with an urgent mission to reach the president.

Then he was in the box, alone in the vestibule, and became the alert spying observer of Abraham Lincoln outlined against the lighted stage. Then he stepped quickly, fired one well-aimed shot, and became the assassin. He grappled with Major Rathbone, slashed him with his dagger and broke free—over the balustrade, onto the stage. There, out of the dark box and into the glare of the footlights, who was he? What was he? In at least one flicker of horror or satisfaction he must have known that he was what he had long been reaching for: John Wilkes Booth, the well-known actor, on stage in his most unforgettable appearance.

And he had words for that instant. "Sic semper tyrannis!" Thus ever to tyrants. The words are Latin; they have a classical ring to them. They might have been spoken by a Brutus. Some observers, including Booth in a later diary entry, reported that he uttered these words while still in the box. Some said he shouted something else, like "Revenge!" But nine of

the eleven witnesses who heard the Latin motto heard it after Booth had
left the box (Bryan, p. 219), and so it is always remembered—as a proclamation from the stage. The words are the state motto of Virginia, adopted
in 1776. They resound with republican virtues from early America as
well as from ancient Rome. They smack of Patrick Henry: "Caesar had
his Brutus—Charles the First, his Cromwell—and George the Third . . . *may
profit by their example. If this* be treason, make the most of it." And of
Thomas Jefferson: "The tree of liberty must be refreshed from time to
time with the blood of patriots and tyrants. It is their natural manure."
And of a revolution by violence to undo the domination of a king.

The words are also part of the Virginia state seal, and so they appeared
where Booth had often seen them—on the pages of the Richmond *Daily
Whig.* Both the seal and the motto had been adopted in 1776, most probably
at the suggestion of the classically trained George Wythe. The figures on
the obverse of the seal are those of a tyrant fallen under the heel of Virtus,
the personification of the Roman ideal of courage and self-sacrifice. Such
figures were derived from the scholarly investigations of Joseph Spence,
an eighteenth-century scholar, critic, and friend of Alexander Pope. His
*Polymetis: or, an Enquiry concerning the Agreement between the Works
of the Roman Poets, and the Remains of the Ancient Artists* (1747) provided
careful descriptions and illustrations of Libertas, Ceres, and Aeternitas (who
appear on the reverse of the Virginia seal) as well as Fortitudo, another
name for courage, in much the same costume and pose that Virtus has
on the seal. The first official description of the seal plainly prescribes an
image of accomplished triumph over tyranny:

> To be engraved on the GREAT SEAL:
> VIRTUS, the genius of the commonwealth, dressed like an *Amazon,*
> resting on a spear with one hand, and holding a sword in the other,
> and treading on TYRANNY, represented by a man prostrate, a crown
> fallen from his head, a broken chain in his left hand, and a scourge
> in his right.
> In the exergon, the word VIRGINIA over the head of VIRTUS; and
> underneath, the words *Sic semper tyrannis.*[15]

Three associations should be noted in this image. The figures are Roman,
with Roman weapons and Roman dress, over a Latin motto. The figure of
Virtus is a woman, "Dressed like an Amazon," and identified with the "genius"
or guiding spirit of the commonwealth. The name Virginia is thus
translated away from monarchy and conquest in the time of Elizabeth I

(the Virgin Queen) and given to a more ancient figure of republican strength. And this Virtus or Virginia carries a sword and spear over the fallen image of a tyrant. The whole thus symbolizes the revolution of 1776 and alludes to the revolutions of Junius Brutus against the Tarquins, in behalf of republican virtue, and of Marcus Brutus against Caesar. Booth might well have supposed that whoever knew Virginia, just across the Potomac from Washington, should have recognized this imagery at once as he raised his dagger and cried out these words.

Did Booth ponder this motto through weeks of plotting and rehearsal? Or did it come to him in a lucky stroke of inspiration? It hardly matters. He said it. He recovered himself from a fall that broke his leg. He rose and spoke and so left an immediate, full expression quite adequate to his sense of his deed, before he fled out into the back alley where his horse was still being attended.

There is a story that as Booth was still hobbling toward the rear door of the theater a lawyer from the front rows of the orchestra seats clambered onto the stage, then pursued him out to the alley and tried to hold him after he was mounted. This was J. B. Stewart, said to be the tallest man in Washington. Whether he actually caught hold of Booth has been disputed.[16] But this image also has its power: a Lincolnesque giant striding after the assassin, just as the ghost of Caesar pursued his murderers in Shakespeare's drama.

After this moment, Booth's remaining words and actions seem faint and crippled. His letter to the *National Intelligencer* never arrived. John Matthews later gave sworn testimony that he took it home with him—to the same house where Lincoln lay dying—tore it open, read it, and burned it. Booth had earlier tried to draw Matthews into the abduction plot, and he remained skittish for the rest of his life about any mention of the Lincoln murder. The best Matthews could recall was that the last paragraph of the letter mentioned a sudden change of plans and that Booth had signed the names of three accomplices after his own (Bryan, p. 202). This hearsay evidence, on balance, indicates at most that Booth wrote some sort of letter to the press and that Matthews had something to do with its disappearance.

Days later in southern Maryland, Booth saw newspaper accounts of the murder and realized that his letter had not been published. He then jotted a hasty explanation into the memorandum book he was carrying. This entry, backdated to "April 13—14," seems intended to correct the misinformation the press was circulating:

Until to day nothing was ever *thought* of sacrificing to our country's wrongs. For six months we had worked to capture. But our cause being almost lost, something decisive & great must be done. But its failure was owing to others, who did not strike for their country with a heart. I struck boldly and not as the papers say. I walked with a firm step through a thousand of his friends, was stopped, but pushed on. A colonel was at his side. I shouted Sic semper *before* I fired. In jumping broke my leg. I passed all his pickets, rode sixty miles that night with the bone of my leg tearing the flesh at every jump. I can never repent it, though we hated to kill. Our country owed all her trouble to him, and God simply made me the instrument of his punishment. The country is not what it *was*. This forced union is not what I have loved. I care not what becomes of me. I have no desire to out-live my country. This night (before the deed), I wrote a long article and left it for the Editors of the National Inteligencer, in which I fully set forth our reasons for our proceedings. He or the Govmt[17]

Here this entry breaks off. The next entry, quoted earlier, complains that Booth was pushed to starvation and despair. "And why? For doing what Brutus was honored for. What made Tell a hero." Later it picks up the point that ended the previous entry: "The little, the very little I left behind to clear my name, the Govmt will not allow to be printed. So ends all." A few lines later Booth shows a flash of bravado: "To night I will once more try the river [i.e., the Potomac] with the intent to cross, though I have a greater desire and almost a mind to return to Washington and in a measure clear my name, which I feel I can do." But by this point he is hardly in control of what he is saying. Hunted, in pain, tired, disappointed, wronged, he writhes on the page and cannot manage a convincing appearance of Roman fortitude or coherent conscience.

I do not repent the blow I struck. I may before my God but not to man.

I think I have done well, though I am abandoned, with the curse of Cain upon me. When if the world knew my heart, *that one* blow would have made me great, though I did desire no greatness.

To night I try to escape these blood hounds once more. Who, who can read his fate. God's will be done.

I have too great a soul to die like a criminal. O may he, may he spare me that and let me die bravely.

I bless the entire world. Have never hated or wronged anyone. This last was not a wrong, unless God deems it so. And its with him to damn or bless me. And for this brave boy with me [David Herold, the accomplice who joined Booth and stayed with him till the barn at Garrett's farm was surrounded] who often prays (yes, before and since) with a true and sincere heart, was it crime in him, if so why can he pray the same[?] I do not wish to shed a drop of blood, but "I must fight the course." 'Tis all that's left me.

(Bryan, pp. 302-3)

This is not like Brutus but like the wallowing Claudius who tries to pray but cannot after recognizing his murder of the elder Hamlet, which marked him, too, with "the curse of Cain":

> O, my offense is rank, it smells to heaven,
> It hath the primal eldest curse upon't,
> A brother's murther. Pray can I not,
> Though inclination be as sharp as will.
> My stronger guilt defeats my strong intent,
> And, like a man to double business bound,
> I stand in pause where I shall first begin,
> And both neglect.
>
> . . . .
>
> And what's in prayer but this twofold force,
> To be forestalled ere we come to fall,
> Or pardon'd being down? then I'll look up.
> My fault is past, but, O, what form of prayer
> Can serve my turn? "Forgive me my foul murther"?
> That cannot be, since I am still possess'd
> Of those effects for which I did the murther.[18]

Booth quite correctly surmised that the government was trying to suppress his claims to fame or heroism; but it was not a thoroughgoing effort. There were futile orders to stop the widespread sale of Booth's photograph; later on the War Department kept his body well hidden and finally allowed its burial in an obscure grave (Bryan, pp. 285-86; Kimmel, pp. 280-81). Soon after the assassination other members of the Booth family were arrested and their papers were seized. A packet that Wilkes left with Asia contained several letters. One was to the Booths' mother; it was taken and did not appear again until it was discovered in government archives in 1977.[19] But another letter was designed as a public explanation, probably to be found and printed when he carried out his abduction plot. It is dated 1864. This paper was released to the press and printed in the Philadelphia

newspapers soon after the assassination. So Booth did get this much opportunity to express his developed motives.

After four years, his letter claims, all hope of restoration of the Union
he loved has perished. He defends opposition to Lincoln and his invasion
of southern rights and institutions. He defends secession. He extols white
supremacy, as both wise and constitutional. In a few sentences he waxes
eloquent. "People of the North," he cries, "to hate tyranny, to love liberty
and justice, to strike out at wrong and oppression, was the teaching of our
fathers. The study of our early history will not let me forget it, and may
it never." He insists that the inflictions upon the South have justified a
war as noble as the American Revolution. "*Even* should we allow they
were wrong at the beginning of this contest, *cruelty and injustice* have
made the wrong become *the right*, and they stand now (before the wonder
and admiration of the world) as a noble band of patriotic heroes. Hereafter,
reading of their deeds, Thermopylae will be forgotten." Over his signature,
Booth identifies himself as "A Confederate doing duty upon his own
responsibility."[20]

All this sounds very lofty. But these are selective quotations. The letter
also lapses into boastfulness and self-pity, into patriotic bombast and weepy
regrets for mother and sisters and flag, into vigorous pledges of self-sacrifice
next to a flat admission that Booth was never on a battlefield. The fault
here may not be that Booth is writing in haste, or in fatigue, or even in
his cups. It may simply be that he had no talent for coherent argument.[21]

Compared to all these more rambling productions, "Sic semper tyrannis!"
is much more effective. It joins word to deed, links both to history, and
refuses to countenance a reply. How different, too, are the reports of Booth's
gasped words after he was shot: "Kill me—kill me," and (to his own
hands) "Useless, useless!" Or his plaintive "Tell mother I die for my
country." The moment on stage catches Booth for just about as long as he
could hold together a lofty identity merged with a line better than any
of his own.

This gesture lives in history. It will not fade from American mythology,
as a shrewd poet quickly observed. Fifteen years after Lincoln's death Walt
Whitman still found it fascinating. He recomposed the scene as he thought
it should have been, and so handed on to many readers the mistaken
impression that he was personally present in the theater at the time.
Whitman's version gathers up many of the well-known details of Booth's
act and interprets them as a "tableau" that rightly symbolizes the end of
the Civil War and a new birth of American identity.

Whitman sees Booth's sudden leap from the state box as a kind of birth or emergence of a new form of life: "in point of fact the main thing, the actual murder, transpired with the quiet and simplicity of any commonest occurrence — the bursting of a bud or pod in the growth of vegetation, for instance." The description that follows requires full and uninterrupted quotation:

> Through the general hum following the stage pause, with the change of positions, came the muffled sound of a pistol-shot, which not one-hundredth part of the audience heard at the time — and yet a moment's hush — somehow, surely, a vague startled thrill — and then, through the ornamented, draperied, starr'd and striped space-way of the President's box, a sudden figure, a man, raises himself with hands and feet, stands a moment on the railing, leaps below to the stage, (a distance of perhaps fourteen or fifteen feet), falls out of position, catching his boot-heel in the copious drapery, (the American flag,) falls on one knee, quickly recovers himself, rises as if nothing had happen'd, (he really sprains his ankle, but unfelt then) — and so the figure, Booth, the murderer, dress'd in plain black broadcloth, bare-headed, with full, glossy, raven hair, and his eyes like some mad animal's flashing with light and resolution, yet with a certain strange calmness, holds aloft in one hand a large knife — walks along not much back from the footlights — turns fully toward the audience his face of statuesque beauty, lit by those basilisk eyes, flashing with desperation, perhaps insanity — launches out in a firm and steady voice the words *Sic semper tyrannis* — and then walks with neither slow nor very rapid pace diagonally across to the back of the stage, and disappears.[22]

Whitman here captures a strange beauty in this performance, and he goes on to acknowledge that this is a deliberate effect. "The main things" about the incident, he insists, have come out over time, emerged from the details of the moment, and risen above the assassination's political or historical significance. "The immeasurable value and meaning of that whole tragedy lies, to me, in senses finally dearest to a nation, (and here all her own) — the imaginative and artistic senses — the literary and dramatic ones" (p. 507). Whitman's sense of poetic value seems to chime with Booth's grasp of high drama. But Whitman is not merely framing Booth and Lincoln here in a tidy talk for a literary salon. He also sees into this event with his own direct experience of the costs of the war — his own years of nursing the torn bodies of soldiers, and witnessing with

his nostrils their suffering and dying and disintegration. Much of his
poetry is an effort to do justice to such grim death. Now he assumes the
mighty authority of having been through it all when he sums up:

> A long and varied series of contradictory events arrives at last at its
> highest poetic, single, central, pictorial denouement. The whole in-
> volved, baffling, multiform whirl of the secession period comes to a
> head, and is gather'd in one brief flash of lightning-illumination —
> one simple, fierce deed. Its sharp culmination, and as it were solution,
> of so many bloody and angry problems, illustrates those climax-
> moments on the stage of universal Time, where the historic Muse
> at one entrance, and the tragic Muse at the other, suddenly ringing
> down the curtain, close an immense act in the long drama of creative
> thought, and give it radiation, tableau, stranger than fiction. Fit ra-
> diation — fit close!
>
> (p. 508)

Whitman does not quite credit Booth with this achievement. He makes
Booth a part of the spectacle, but the central figure is Lincoln; and Lincoln
in turn is an embodiment of the American people. His dramatic death is
for Whitman a mystery of American unity and identity. "The final use
of a heroic-eminent life — especially of a heroic-eminent death — is its
indirect filtering into the nation and the race, and to give, often at many
removes, but unerringly, age after age, color and fibre to the personalism
of the youth and maturity of that age and of mankind."[23] These words
almost match the famous lines in *Hamlet* about the whole purpose of
acting: "whose end, both at the first and now, was and is, to hold as 'twere
the mirror up to nature: to show virtue her feature, scorn her own image,
and the very age and body of the time his form and pressure" (3.2.21-24).
But Whitman argues that an actual heroic death reaches beyond immediate
reflection of individuals or an age, to shape a permanent national identity.
"Then there is a cement to the whole people, subtler, more underlying,
than any thing in written constitution, or courts or armies — namely,
the cement of a death identified thoroughly with that people, at its head,
and for its sake" (p. 508). Thus Lincoln's death is the last necessary touch
of the war, the final gesture Lincoln could make to raise America to a
place among nations:

> How the imagination — how the student loves these things! America,
> too, is to have them. For not in all great deaths, nor far or near —
> not Caesar in the Roman senate-house, or Napoleon passing away in
> the wild night-storm at St. Helena — not Paleologus, falling, desperately

fighting, piled over dozens deep with Grecian corpses—not calm old Socrates, drinking the hemlock—outvies that terminus of the secession war, in one man's life, there in our midst, in our own time—that seal of the emancipation of three million slaves—that parturition and delivery of our at last really free Republic, born again, henceforth to commence its career of genuine homogeneous Union, compact, consistent with itself.

(p. 508)

Here the recognition is explicit: As in Rome, so in America—a death to give depth and meaning to a national identity. And here, like Booth, Whitman is forced to borrow fit terms for his central image. Lincoln at Gettysburg had described "fathers" who "brought forth" a new nation, "conceived" in liberty, and he called for a dedication to a "new birth" of freedom. Now Whitman celebrates "that parturition and delivery of our at last really free Republic." But by seeing birth in death Whitman also tangles himself in a vision more complicated than the gospel he seems almost breathless to proclaim. For his earlier passage is too vivid in what it implies. Out of the "starr'd and striped space-way of the President's box" came and emerged an assassin—a democratic power as monstrous as it was beautiful ("his face of statuesque beauty, lit by those basilisk eyes").

The celebrated democratic poet thus ponders the most significant event of his time—and stops short. Whitman sees its full tragic dimension, but records it in imagery that swells against his tamer, patriotic argument. In the one minute that Booth stood in the box with Lincoln he held out a petty pistol and fired a mean blast against all American order. His act may have ennobled Lincoln, but it also caught him forever in a swirl of tawdry American theatrical crime: "in the midst of that pandemonium, infuriated soldiers, the audience and the crowd, the stage and all its actors and actresses, its paint pots, spangles, and gas-lights" (Whitman, p. 507). In the minute that followed, Booth changed places with the president. He stood triumphant—making the stage his political platform, crying his classical cry, reechoing the sentiments of every revolutionary—and escaped on horseback. But Lincoln lay as defeated as a man can be, revealed as mortal in a hollow and frail shell of public appearances—in that box now raised like a stage above the stage. Booth's shot remains a blast against Lincoln's deepest creed that all men are created equal. It asserts that a wild Booth was the equal of a deeply thoughtful Lincoln — was, in a sense, his necessary and inescapable companion. It justifies Lincoln's exercise of armed might, by turning it back upon him through Booth's steady hand.[24] It imprints these morals, too, upon the American memory. It brings down the curtain on a classical stage of American democracy under a peacefully deliberated Constitution, and brings up the houselights on characters still in costumes and greasepaint, striving futilely to direct a bewildered and leaderless crowd.

7

Edwin Booth as Hamlet

*E*DWIN BOOTH was acting in Boston when Lincoln was assassinated. The theater manager immediately canceled his next appearance, and Booth readily agreed. For the moment, and for months afterward, it seemed that his brother's act had finished Edwin's career on stage. But by the following January he had summoned the courage to return to New York in the role of Hamlet. At least one newspaper, the New York *Herald*, expressed a predictable outrage at the idea:

Is the Assassination of Caesar to be Performed? — The public must be surprised to learn that a Booth is to appear on the New York stage the coming week. We know not which is the most worthy of condemnation, the heartless cupidity of the foreign manager, who has no real sympathy with this country or the feelings of the American people, in bringing out this actor at the present time, or the shocking bad taste of the actor himself in appearing. Will he appear as the assassin of Caesar? That would be, perhaps, the most suitable character and the most sensational one to answer the manager's purpose. Shame upon such indecent and reckless disregard of propriety and the sentiments of the American people! Can the sinking fortunes of this foreign manager be sustained in no other way than by such an indecent violation of propriety? The blood of our martyred President is not yet dry in the memory of the people, and the very name of the assassin is appalling to the public mind; still a Booth is advertised to appear before a New York audience![1]

But other newspapers replied to this attack, the house was filled with well-wishers, and at Hamlet's appearance they cheered and welcomed the well-known star.[2] Edwin Booth, after all, had always been an upright defender of the Union. He could not be held personally responsible for the behavior of a wild younger brother. Besides, he made an excellent Hamlet, which audiences were still eager to see. By January 22, 1867, the actor's critics had been routed. A large and distinguished delegation came forward that night after the final curtain to present Booth with a Tiffany gold medal in commemoration of his hundred nights in *Hamlet* in 1864-65.

The shame of the assassination still pursued the Booths. Asia and her husband moved to England in 1868, and she never returned. Junius found a way to go on as a theater manager and occasional actor. Edwin resumed his career. But the memory of John Wilkes remained an open wound. Edwin never again performed in Washington, though he was invited by letters from many distinguished people there, including President Arthur. Edwin was the best-known, richest, and best-connected member of the family. And his quick action in a railway mishap may have saved Robert Lincoln, the president's oldest son, just a month or two before the president was killed.[3] He therefore wrote on behalf of the family to obtain his brother's body and seized effects. From a distance he did his duty about a proper reburial. In New York he sorted and burned the trunk of theatrical costumes and effects. Nobody ever touched the money the assassin had left in Canadian banks; but Edwin took on the responsibility of dealing with the Garrett family, whose barn had been burned in his brother's capture.[4] Meanwhile the press went on reviving old stories and mentioning the assassin when discussing the living actors related to him. Edwin was to be upset by such publicity for decades, even in faraway countries.[5] Once he even got a request for free tickets from Boston Corbett, the sergeant who claimed to have killed his brother.[6] Edwin kept a photograph of John, but he rarely spoke of him even among intimates; among others he evaded any approach to the subject.

All the Booths had plenty of other worries and upsetting memories if they paused to consider them, and Edwin in particular had a life of heavy sorrows. The assassination took its place among many regrettable legends. There were the elder Junius's hard drinking and bouts of wild behavior, and his elopement with Mary Ann Holmes (the actors' mother) while he

was still married to another woman. There were the younger Junius's
years in California with a common-law wife. There were plenty of theatrical misadventures by actors who were too young, too inexperienced,
or too drunk for their parts.

Edwin Booth was to carry his share of these woes, plus many of his
own. As a boy he had been his father's companion on his travels, charged
with looking out for that difficult but lovable older man. As a young man
he had his rough apprenticeship on the road. And his adult years were
burdened with grief. Mary Devlin, Edwin's first wife, died in 1863, just
two years after they were married, leaving a daughter just over a year old.
She died suddenly of illness at their home in Dorchester, Massachusetts,
while Edwin was acting (and drinking heavily) in New York; he was
summoned by telegram, but arrived too late.[7] Mary McVicker, his much
younger second wife, lost a child in 1870 after a wretched delivery and
thereafter became possessive; she died insane in 1881. The McVickers, a
theatrical family in Chicago, blamed Edwin for her decline, as well as for
his falling into a financial muddle from which he had to be rescued. After
losing the Winter Garden Theater to fire in 1867, Booth had projected an
even grander showplace, the costly and elaborate Booth's Theatre, which
opened in 1869. But he was swindled by a succession of partners, eventually
lost the theater, and was forced into bankruptcy after the Panic of 1873.
For years he maintained a heavy touring schedule to keep even with
enormous debts. Eventually, he earned his way out of them; he finally
settled with all his creditors in 1877.[8] But his troubles were far from over.
A carriage accident in 1875 crippled and permanently disfigured his left
hand and forearm. In 1879 he was on stage in Chicago when a crazed
man fired at him from a balcony; he was to carry the bullet on his watch
chain for the rest of his life. By the time Edwin came to solid prosperity
his health was failing. He lived until 1893 and died well loved by a large
public. But his was a hard life, a life of misfortunes amplified in many
a popular biography.

Edwin Booth survived all these setbacks by going on as a seasoned actor.
The theater was what he had been born to, and it remained the only
means of livelihood he knew. Offstage he was a gentle, generous friend
but hardly a dynamic character. He was embarrassed even by the necessity
of saying a few words when receiving a public honor. His letters show
that he was neither learned nor deeply intellectual by nature; he acknowledged these limitations and often tried to get around them with a forced
heartiness: puns, clichés, wrenched tag lines, and deliberate solecisms. His

financial disasters show he had a poor sense of money and business. But on stage he could be a masterful presence. He was not large in stature, nor ruggedly handsome. He was weak in comedy and never quite convincing as a young lover. He joked that his Romeo was the role that made people laugh. But in a handful of tragic roles he projected a steady power. He concentrated on this repertory, especially Bulwer-Lytton's *Richilieu* and the best known tragedies of Shakespeare. He became and remained the most celebrated American Hamlet of the nineteenth century.

To thousands he *was* Hamlet. John Wilkes is reported to have confided that Edwin not only played the role, he lived it: "No, no, no! There's but one Hamlet to my mind; that's my brother Edwin. You see, between ourselves, he *is* Hamlet—melancholy and all." This legendary judgment was published in a memoir by Clara Morris long after John and Edwin had both died (Ruggles, p. 170). But it expressed a feeling of many who were close to Edwin. His sister Asia said much the same thing when she summed up Edwin's quiet reserve despite years of misfortune in just one line from the play: "I have that within which passeth show" (*EYB*, p. 163). Many contemporary critics reechoed the idea in their reviews; many friends repeated it in their reminiscences. "We of today live in the era of Booth; and Booth, to a majority of us, is Hamlet."[9] And a sober theater historian, critically weighing the exaggerations of past observers, must still conclude that Booth's Hamlet commanded worship. " 'Worship' is not too strong a word to describe the responses of Booth's following. . . . Booth, . . . however vividly he shone on the public scene, was an innocent; wrapped in Art and the Ideal, he was insulated from corruption. He would have made the Theatre a school and a temple as well as a playhouse, and he strove with priestly devotion to make his Hamlet an idol of virtue. For many thousands of playgoers it was a lesson and a rite" (*HEB*, p. xv).

Obviously, Booth became a very complex Hamlet, despite his seeming innocence in private life. In some ways he seemed born to the role; but it could also be a public identity he bore dutifully, or a long-term commitment that he used to mask his personal life. It was a role to draw audiences out in shared sorrow and wonder over the human condition— especially when they recognized Booth's own life of sorrows deepening Hamlet's penetrating eyes. Among those sorrows was the crime of John Wilkes Booth—a crime against the country, against the Booth family, against the possibility of dignity in the theater.

Exactly how Edwin absorbed that outrage and answered it with his art has never been fully analyzed. Perhaps it cannot be disentangled from many other strands in his long career. The invaluable, patient reconstruction by Charles H. Shattuck treats Edwin's career and the assassination as completely separate matters; *The Hamlet of Edwin Booth* mentions John only three times, very incidentally. But Edwin's Hamlet did answer John's Brutus, just as surely as those two roles answered each other in Shakespeare's consecutive tragedies. And the most thorough records of the later Hamlet performances leave no doubt: assassination and its consequences were what Edwin Booth ritualized night after night. And in his own special way he drew from that part an extraordinary epiphany of law.

According to a family legend, Edwin first played Hamlet because his father thought he looked the part. When they were acting in San Francisco, Edwin wore a black costume for a different role on a benefit night. His father remarked: "You look like Hamlet; why do you not act *Hamlet* for your benefit?" Edwin replied, "If I ever have another, I *will*" (*EYB*, p. 131). Whether or not this story is true, it points to an early recognition of the traditional Hamlet in the young Edwin's dark features. In 1870, when Edwin was thirty-six, he still appeared perfect for the role. "His spare and almost attenuated frame, his thoughtful, and, indeed, habitually mournful expression; his hollow, low-pitched voice; his splendid dark eye; his jetty disheveled locks, and a certain morbidness that is suggested by his whole look and bearing, carry conviction to the mass of beholders that in him they see as near an approach as possible to the Hamlet of Shakespeare." So wrote an anonymous but judicious critic for the *New York Times*, reviewing the most elaborate production Booth was to mount.[10] And photographs, especially the Sarony portraits of Booth as Hamlet, confirm this judgment.

His father had died before Edwin first played the role, so the young actor was touched from the beginning with a burden of genuine mourning. He had learned his art from his father. He began to make his way on the strength of his father's name. Then, and throughout his life, he was to carry the memory of his father on stage, just as young Hamlet carried the memory of old Hamlet. His sister Asia cites lines from the play as if they in fact echoed twice in Edwin's mind when he first performed the role.

> The words once spoken carelessly to his father had assumed the sacredness of a promise: —
> > "Thy commandment all alone shall live
> > Within the book and volume of my brain
> > Unmixed with baser matter."

One can imagine with what intensity of feeling, as he thought of his father, he spoke the lines, which had acquired for him a powerful significance, —

> "He was a man, take him for all in all,
> I shall not look upon his like again."
>
> (*EYB*, p. 137)

Asia quotes lines that come early in the play (1.5.102-4 and 1.2.187-88); they must have been especially difficult for a young actor nervously attempting this role before audiences that knew his father. Shattuck has traced influences of Junius upon Edwin's Hamlet that would endure to the end. The young actor talked about his father often. He made him so vivid to his first wife that she sometimes believed his spirit spoke to her. After her death, Edwin visited spiritualists and was almost sure he received messages from her and from his father. On stage he sometimes fancied he heard his own father's voice in the voice of the ghost. As Hamlet, he wore a neck chain with a portrait of the dead king; the image he actually carried was a miniature of the elder Booth (*HEB*, pp. 5-6).

But Edwin's earliest performance was a departure from the kind of acting the elder Booth had practiced. The difference was noticed and appreciated even then by a highly intelligent newspaper critic. Ferdinand C. Ewer had observed and reviewed the young actor in many minor roles; he watched and eagerly praised him when he assumed his father's famous role as Richard III and warmed to it late in the play. Four nights later Edwin took his benefit as Hamlet, and again Ewer was alert to his special talent. To Ewer, the ideal Hamlet was a flexible, easy gentleman, quite unlike the melodramatic figure of thundering old-fashioned tragedians or the cold and unbending Hamlet of other current stars. "Melancholy without gloom, contemplative yet without misanthropy, philosophical yet enjoying play-fulness in social converse, a man by himself yet with ardent feelings of friendship, a thorough knower of human nature, Hamlet stands as the type of all that is firm, dignified, gentlemanly and to be respected in a man."[11] Booth at the age of nineteen could not be all this, as Ewer frankly noted. But the critic saw that with all his faults Edwin came closer to realizing this ideal than any other actor of the time. Ewer saw the promise of a great Hamlet in Booth, and Booth rejoiced to see his conception of Hamlet reflected in Ewer's prose. The actor kept and studied this passage for years and later wrote to its author for another copy.

This flexible, gentlemanly ideal was different from the elder Booth's style. But Edwin still carried a heritage of his father's inner fire. Father and son both had to make their careers by traveling from town to town and meeting expectations of an electrifying performance from a star. Edwin had to be melodramatic, and in many roles he proved he could be. Richard Lockridge has briefly but deftly described this situation. Shakespeare, he explains, was always the "inner citadel" of the actor's repertoire.

> The other plays were, by all modern standards, extremely bad. But they had one thing in common: each of them had a central character of satisfactory importance and the proper purple patches of which the actors could make "points." One of the best of these, as an example, is found in *Richelieu*:
>
>   Mark, where she stands!—around her form I draw
>   The awful circle of our solemn church!
>   Set but a foot within that holy ground,
>   And on thy head—yea, though it wore a crown—
>   I launch the curse of Rome!
>
> It was for such moments that the older tragedians played. For those fine outbursts they husbanded their strength, walking softly, even listlessly, through the routine of the play, drawing themselves up when they saw a "point" approaching. Most of them were not at all averse to striding down stage at such moments, facing the audience, and letting the pit and gallery have it full force.
>
> (Lockridge, p. 38)

To meet this taste, Edwin kept Bulwer-Lytton's *Richelieu* (1839) as his second-favorite role (*HEB*, p. 40). But he developed Hamlet as something different, a distinct role for his peculiar talents. It represented an ideal that he would need years to perfect before he could bring it before a properly cultivated audience, the new, more refined and exclusive audience that developed in the later nineteenth century.

The older acting style lingered for a generation. It was still a standard by which a star was measured. And it was still an indelible memory associated with the Booths.

Walt Whitman, for example, admired Edwin Booth but found that he "had everything but guts."[12] And in that remark he was definitely comparing the son to the father. Whitman had seen Junius often in the later 1830s, and he could never forget him. He saw him at the Bowery Theater, which was then a New York showplace, frequented by "the leading authors, poets, editors, of those times" as well as by several American presidents. This was before it became a cheap and vulgar playhouse in a notorious district. But Whitman describes the audience generally as masculine: "alert, well-dress'd, full blooded young and middle-aged men, the best average of American-born mechanics" who could fill the house with the "electric force and muscle" of their applause. It was in these circumstances that Whitman in 1885 could still recall the way Junius made his entrance as Richard III.

> After a one-act farce over, as contrast and prelude, the curtain rising for the tragedy, I can, from my good seat in the pit, pretty well front, see again Booth's quiet entrance from the side, as, with head bent, he slowly and in silence, (amid the tempest of boisterous hand-clapping,) walks down the stage to the footlights with that peculiar and abstracted gesture, musingly kicking his sword, which he holds off from him by its sash. Though fifty years have pass'd since then, I can hear the clank, and feel the perfect following hush of perhaps three thousand people waiting. (I never saw an actor who could make more of the said hush or wait, and hold the audience in an indescribable, half-delicious, half-irritating suspense.) And so throughout the entire play, all parts, voice, atmosphere, magnetism from
> > "Now is the winter of our discontent,"
> to the closing death fight with Richmond, were of the finest and grandest. The latter character was play'd by a stalwart young fellow named Ingersoll. Indeed, all the renderings were wonderfully good. But the great spell cast upon the mass of hearers came from Booth. Especially was the dream scene very impressive. A shudder went through every nervous system in the audience; it certainly did through mine.[13]

Whitman concludes that this kind of performance was an old and dying art form, but it found its great climax in Booth.

> Yes; although Booth must be class'd in that antique, almost extinct school, inflated, stagy, rendering Shakspere (perhaps inevitably, appropriately) from the growth of arbitrary and often cockney conventions, his genius was to me one of the grandest revelations of my life, a lesson of artistic expression. The words fire, energy, *abandon*, found in him unprecedented meanings. I never heard a speaker or actor who could give such a sting to hauteur or the taunt. I never heard from any other the charm of unswervingly perfect vocalization without trenching at all on mere melody, the province of music.
>
> (Whitman, p. 597)

These words are an astonishing testament if they mean what they say — that Booth's acting was a lesson of artistic expression and abandon for the great American singer of self. They are notable, too, for what they reveal about Whitman's description of Lincoln's assassination, quoted in the last chapter. In Whitman's words, John Wilkes Booth moved along the foot- lights, with his knife aloft, and proclaimed "in a firm and steady voice the words *Sic semper tyrannis*" (Whitman, p. 505). This is obviously another scene of dramatic "point" in the grand old style. In fact, there are several detailed correspondences between Junius in the Bowery and John Wilkes at Ford's, as Whitman describes them: the conspicuous sword on one, the knife held aloft by the other; the unhurried suspense developed by the father, the "strange calmness" of the son; "the great spell cast" by Junius's renderings, the hypnotic eyes of John Wilkes; the hauteur of the old actor's taunts, the sting of "Sic semper tyrannis." And each passage describes what Whitman takes to be the culmination of a long development of historical forces. As we saw earlier, the assassination drew "a long and varied series of contradictory events" to their "highest poetic, single, central, pictorial denouement." For Whitman, Junius Booth provided a passing glimpse into the great Shakespearean tradition. "Booth was royal heir and legitimate representative of the Garrick-Kemble-Siddons dramatic tradi- tions."

> I consider that my seeing the man those years glimps'd for me, beyond all else, that inner spirit and form — that unquestionable charm and vivacity, but intrinsic sophistication and artificiality — crystallizing rapidly upon the English stage and literature at and after Shakspere's time, and coming on accumulatively through the seventeenth and eighteenth centuries to the beginning, fifty or forty years ago, of those disintegrating, decomposing processes now authoritatively going on.
> (Whitman, pp. 596-97)

Whitman concludes his recollection of Junius Booth with the words Shakespeare gives Mark Antony over the body of Brutus: "Though those brilliant years had many fine and even magnificent actors, undoubtedly at Booth's death (1852) went the last and by far the noblest Roman of them all" (Whitman, p. 597). Was John Wilkes, then, his father's true heir? Or was Whitman's memory of drama forever impressed and con- ditioned by what he witnessed at the Bowery, so that he composed even Lincoln's murder to match that imagery?

As we have seen, Edwin Booth worked hard to grow beyond his father's fame and his father's standards and to distance himself from them. He developed a more supple, less histrionic acting style in his Hamlet. And when he came to New York he tried both literally and figuratively to establish himself far uptown from the Bowery. By the 1850s many men and women prided themselves on a more genteel taste, an appreciation of finer, gentler, more exquisite forms of art. Edwin's first bids for stardom in the eastern cities were helped by that new taste as much as by his father's reputation. An 1857 review of *Richard III* exactly catches the fine balance he was managing: "He omits many opportunities for making technical points and slips over many sentences which, in other hands, have seldom failed to gain the audible approval of the house; but, on the other hand, when he takes up a favorite scene with the resolve to make it a sensation, all his tameness instantly vanishes and he renders the passage with a vigorous truthfulness which startles his audience into wild enthusiasm and brings down a perfect storm of applause."[14] There was encouragement awaiting such a blend of power and restraint. Audiences not only applauded Edwin but welcomed him. In Boston several leading citizens and Harvard students petitioned the theater for a repeat performance of *Hamlet* (*HEB*, p. 12). Newspapers praised him and sometimes cited his performances in a campaign to put down the style of the aging Edwin Forrest. And before long Edwin found more forceful support in the form of constant coaching from new companions.

In June 1857 he received a letter from Adam Badeau, a young New York journalist and connoisseur. Badeau had been following the actor's performances; he now introduced himself and exhorted Booth to visit him and learn from him. Charles Shattuck has fully discussed the results of this introduction. Badeau and Booth spent much of the summer together and became steady friends and correspondents. Badeau was something of a dandy, and he evidently felt a homosexual attraction to Booth. But Booth seems to have had his own longing for what Badeau could offer: confirmation of his talent from a lively intellectual. Badeau introduced the actor to many pictorial artists in New York. He urged him to read critics like Hazlitt, Goethe, and Georges Sand. He took him to libraries and galleries to teach him about authentic periods and styles. He lectured to him to control his drinking and to learn French. He assured him that he belonged among the most sophisticated New Yorkers and proposed him as a member of the Century Club. This friendship went on for years as a force in Booth's life, a pressure of high expectation. And it may have had important effects in the way it cooled — when Badeau went into the army in 1861, developed an infatuation for another soldier, and later became the devoted aide and biographer of Ulysses S. Grant. Badeau's army service drew the actor into personal sympathy for the Union cause; he and John Wilkes actually nursed Badeau at Booth's New York house after he was seriously wounded in 1863. And as Badeau rose to a general's rank, his career must have challenged Booth to fulfill his own destiny. It is an odd match of characters, anyhow, that at Edwin's wedding in 1860 the best man was Adam Badeau and Booth's other witness was his brother John Wilkes.[15]

By that marriage he gained an even stronger nurturing ally, the great love of his life, Mollie Devlin. She first met him by playing Juliet to his Romeo in 1856 — when she was sixteen and he was twenty-three. According to the comic actor Joseph Jefferson, Mollie had been placed in the Jeffersons' care as a young girl, to earn money for her destitute family; it was Jefferson who brought her and Booth together.[16] But when their paths crossed again she proved to be much more than a pretty young waif. For a year before their marriage Booth set her up in an apartment in New Jersey, with books, a piano, a pair of tutors, and instructions to improve her mind while he was on tour. In return she wrote him letters of criticism and instruction, and after they were married she continued to keep a notebook of criticisms to support his development. She was his darling, but she was also his more studious and articulate artistic conscience, as Shattuck shows by quoting from her many surviving letters. A few lines from one of them sum up her clearheaded idealism: "God bless you, my future ambition, will be to see you, great, and good and if, devotion of mind, and intellect, but what is still more influencing and absorbing — affection — can accomplish it you shall be everything, that the world has predicted."[17]

Mollie supported Edwin through a season of mixed reviews in 1860-61 in New York. She accompanied him to England for a badly planned season the following year; their daughter was born in London in December. But back in America, Mollie did not survive another winter. She died suddenly of pneumonia in February 1863; she was not yet twenty-three. She was gone, and Booth was left with a deepened melancholy; a tiny daughter to care for; a heavy sense of guilt and longing (partly assuaged by visits to spiritualist mediums); and the burden of knowing he was not yet all that she had wanted him to become. But even in death she remained a strengthening influence. "Oh, that I could give you the full companionship of that love as I have felt it since Mary's death," Booth once wrote to a woman whose husband died in battle in 1862. And a few months later he added: "I feel that all my actions have been and are influenced by her whose love is to me the strength and wisdom of my spirit. Whatever I may do of serious import, I regard it as a performance of a sacred duty I owe to all that is pure and honest in my nature — a duty to the very religion of my heart."[18]

Booth returned to the stage in the fall of 1863, opening again in *Hamlet*. By late 1864 he was ready to launch his famous production at the Winter Garden in New York — elaborately prepared with new "historically accurate" sets. This was the Hundred Nights *Hamlet* that ran until late March 1865.

By the time of Lincoln's assassination, therefore, the pattern of Edwin's career and public identity had already been permanently set. The shock of his brother's crime could not change it but was rather absorbed into it. Edwin was Hamlet. He had already become a haunted, noble, gentlemanly Hamlet both on the stage and off. He was more than this and less than this, of course; it was a mask that was, in part, thrust upon him. But Booth was a masquer who had trained to wear it well, as he did for decades. Booth (the name as well as the man) was later to build and manage a great new theater as a showcase for Shakespeare. But already he had mounted *Hamlet* very elaborately at the Winter Garden for a record-breaking run. Booth was later to bring artistic idealism to New York, by building his theater there and by founding The Players, where actors could socialize with leading men in other fields. But already he had found a secure niche among the established New York artists, writers, critics, and patrons. Booth was to become an object of public sentiment, playing Hamlet as a man touched by the sorrows everyone knew he personally had undergone. But by 1865 he had already lived out the role of the son grieving for the irreplaceable father, and had become the bereft young widower. His loss and shame over John Wilkes Booth, like his later financial ruin or troubled marriage or crippling accident, could only be another incident in a life already singled out for suffering. Even as a patriotic figure he was already conspicuous as *the* American tragedian, who had already rivaled European stars in theaters on both sides of the Atlantic.

As we have seen, all the Booths suffered because of John Wilkes's crime. It called up other shames and old wounds; it put them in immediate danger; for years afterward it still brought them insults and threats. But Edwin's career had prepared him very well for just such a blow. His life had almost been one long rehearsal. He was prepared to go on again just as he had twice before, by opening in another production of *Hamlet*. He was practiced at meeting notoriety with silence and reserve. He had labored patiently to meet the most demanding criticism with his impersonation of the greatest of thoughtful good men. He was already overcompensating in order to make the name Booth distinguished because of his particular achievements. He was thus in an extraordinary position in the late 1860s. Instead of crushing him, his brother turned out to be his foil, the villainous contrast to his tempered noble excellence.

And another burden and trial also served in the long run to enhance the effectiveness of his Hamlet. This was the hard fact of his life as an actor, that he had to keep traveling to make money. Booth kept traveling over a period of more than thirty-five years. He traveled with his father, then traveled to establish himself as a star. After he had settled in New York, he traveled abroad to make a bid for international stardom. And back in America he was driven to keep up his name and make a fortune. He had to raise money to start the construction of Booth's Theatre. Once the theater was built, he had to make more money to pay off its mortgage and the costs of its lavish productions, and yet more money to pay off its bottomless debts. Finally he kept on touring to earn the fortune he might have enjoyed years before. As a result Booth came to know America by its rail lines, its hotels, and its gatherings in theaters grand and meager, from coast to coast and from the Great Lakes to the Gulf. He saw them all.

And the people of America turned out to see him. Along with a few other touring stars and platform lecturers like Mark Twain or General Sherman, Booth was one of the most widely seen persons in America in this period. In that sense he was better known than any president. People saved to buy tickets and then traveled miles to see Booth. Thousands of them did it again a year or ten years later. What they came to witness was not only an evening of theater but a larger public event, the appearance of the great American tragedian in both art and life, the actor who had rivaled all other serious stars in America and abroad—and, not least important, the survivor who still rose to the heights of decency after his brother's cruel treason. The burden of making a noble response to a corrupting crime is of course the heart of *Hamlet*. When Booth arrived in town to perform in *Hamlet* he might well have called up deep resonances out of his own life and the nation's.

But were these among the feelings Booth actually stirred? It is hard if not impossible to tell. Most of the thousands who saw him have left no records at all. Newspaper clippings and journal reviews record impressions of the acting or staging of particular plays. Even retrospective studies leave Booth in a peculiar half-light. They describe his extraordinary physical, temperamental, and experiential fitness for the role of Hamlet, but breathe scarcely a word about John Wilkes Booth. What is one to make of such silence? Does it bespeak the decorous taste of high-toned critics and their fastidious readers? Was it a shared deference to Edwin's own silence about his brother? Did Edwin's acting talent fully offset any impulse to reexamine the details of his history? Was the murder of Lincoln too painful or sordid a mystery for the columns of dramatic criticism? Or was the mystique of the suffering of Hamlet so powerful that no one arose to discuss its sources explicitly? Whatever the true balance of these motives, the contemporary records treat the patriotic potential of Booth's Hamlet very faintly. They leave the impression that Edwin Booth lived in one world and John Wilkes Booth in quite another. By late 1871 Edwin could even do what the New York *Herald* in 1866 had flung out as the ultimate outrage: he played Brutus in his own staging of *Julius Caesar*. He even opened this production on Christmas Night, apparently without the faintest ripple of protest.[19]

Such success in a separate career may be the measure of Edwin Booth's achievement. After 1865 his brother's name was certainly not forgotten. John Wilkes Booth remains familiar to this day, while Edwin has receded into the shades of theater history. Edwin was quite aware that there was always a bloodstain ready to spread across the name Booth. If others kept a public silence like his own, and suppressed one Booth's crime with another's deserved fame, so much to the good. That was surely one of the effects for which he was laboring.

Fortunately, however, we are able to see into his theater and into his behavior on stage, as we can see into the work of no other actor before this century. In 1969 Charles Shattuck was able to bring out a very thorough reconstruction of Booth's *Hamlet*, covering its development from 1853 to 1891. Shattuck turned over a wealth of letters, press notices, promptbooks, and set designs and illustrations. And he closely copied a remarkable journal, in which a young theatergoer preserved even Booth's gestures and intonations in the great 1870 performances. Among other things, this journal records exactly how the actor interpreted Hamlet's final murder of the king and its moral implications.

Shattuck stresses that this *Hamlet* was the high point in Booth's development of the role, when Booth was completely in control of his own theater and eager to produce a consummate effect. His theater was new and lavish, with impressive special effects in the auditorium as well as onstage. Heavy fans circulated warm air in winter and cool air in summer up through perforations in the stands under the spectators' chairs. The scenery was not adjusted with flats in grooves moved in by workmen from the wings; it rose magically from deep underground by hydraulic pressure. The scenes were specially created to represent an "authentic" Elsinore of medieval Denmark — with great depths of playing area and surroundings of solid-seeming architecture. And to match these effects, the players were costumed in fine woolen garments; all of them except Booth wore blond wigs.

In short, this was *Hamlet* on a new and spectacular scale — a great event in the New York season. It awed many spectators and critics, but provoked other responses, too. Less stately theaters put on burlesques — with *Hamlet* duels in boxing gloves, or *Hamlet* in Arctic mittens and overshoes, with a star made up to look like a furry Booth at his most melancholy. (Booth went to see the latter and laughed himself to tears.)[20] Even Shakespeare descended from the "Dramatic Sphere, Spiritual World" to publish his own review in the New York *Leader* — rebutting all earlier critics of his play, chastising all earlier productions, and thanking Booth for at last mounting it with all the resources of a better age than the poet's own.[21] Those resources can still be recaptured from a series of watercolor sketches for the scenery of this production, and from an article with eight engravings of the wonders backstage.[22]

This setting was a show in itself. As Shattuck points out, the new effects were so impressive many critics simply forgot that Booth had already staged Hamlet "authentically" at the Winter Garden in 1864-65. A few observers remarked that an "authentic" *Hamlet* was a futile exercise anyhow; Shakespeare's imagination had made an eclectic masterpiece, drawing on many sources and conventions besides those of tenth-century Denmark. For these reasons and others it is hard to agree with Shattuck's central idea: that Booth's "way was to strip a role to its essentials, to seize upon the ideas in it which as a child of mid-century he believed to be valid Shakespearean ideas, and to project them directly, without distracting clutter, to the mind of his audience" (*HEB*, p. 46). This statement makes Booth seem far too deliberate and intellectual as an actor, and far too single-minded as a producer. Some of his contemporaries saw him instead as restless, indefinite, or inconsistent, even in *Hamlet*. And Shattuck elsewhere allows that a wild, inexplicable depth of Booth's personality "was the unique component of his genius."[23]

Nevertheless Booth had a grand and driving desire to make a *Hamlet* worthy of his theater. He even put this ideal into words. He had one of his talented actors prepare a brochure, *Booth's Theatre: Hamlet*, which explained the special preparations for this production. It also told the audience how to respond: the play should lift us "from the narrow sphere of our daily lives into a loftier, grander region, whose atmosphere perforce shall purify and exalt our souls . . . shall infuse some of its own precious metal of nobility, honesty, and courage into our own lives, glorifying our too mundane souls with some of its higher, more heavenly attributes!"[24] The refined ore of nobility, honesty, and courage, of course, lay in Booth's own impersonation of the prince.

And Booth as Hamlet undoubtedly did purify and exalt some spirits in his theater. He appealed, as we have seen, to a new taste in drama. He also appealed to a new kind of audience: not the robust crowd that had roared and stamped and hissed at the performances of his father or Edwin Forrest, but row upon row of separate individuals who now attended to the stage with a serious silence. Silence can hardly be measured as an index of a play's power. But out of that silence came another form of tribute, deliberate personal testaments written up after Booth's performances. Booth inspired at least three notable, private accounts of his acting in *Hamlet*.

Lawrence Levine's recent *Highbrow/Lowbrow* stresses that a new, silent audience was emerging in America not only in theaters but also in concert halls, libraries, galleries, museums, and even in the open, public parks of the later nineteenth century.

> The masterworks of the classic composers were to be performed in their entirety by highly trained musicians on programs free from the contamination of lesser works or lesser genres, free from the interference of audience or performer, free from the distractions of the mundane; audiences were to approach the masters and their works with proper respect and proper seriousness, for aesthetic and spiritual elevation rather than mere entertainment was the goal. This transition [to a new standard of taste] was not confined to the worlds of symphonic or operatic music or of Shakespearean drama; it was manifest in other important areas of expressive culture as well.

And under these conditions the proper, even strictly enforced, response was silence and individual reflection.

> With important exceptions — particularly in the areas of sport and religion — audiences in America had become less interactive, less of a public and more of a group of mute receptors. Art was becoming a one-way process: the artist communicating and the audience receiving. "Silence in the face of art," was becoming the norm and was

helping to create audiences without the independence to pit their taste, publicly at least, against those of critics, performers, and artists. ... The desire of the promoters of the new high culture to convert audiences into a collection of people reacting *individually* rather than collectively, was increasingly realized by the twentieth century. This was achieved partly by fragmenting and segregating audiences so that it was more and more difficult in the twentieth century to find the equivalent of the nineteenth-century theater audience that could serve as a microcosm of the entire society.[25]

Levine mentions Edwin Booth as an actor who strove to cultivate this new audience. In fact, Booth's career perfectly coincided with its development, as sharp observers at the time explicitly noted. One of Booth's steadiest critics was A. C. Wheeler, who wrote for the New York *World* under the pseudonym "Nym Crinkle." Crinkle analyzed Booth's *Hamlet* in 1870, in a long review that opened as follows: "Mr. Booth's *Hamlet* is the perfect expression of the artistic taste of our times. That taste is characterized, and nowhere in so marked a manner as in the drama, by the substitution of finish for feeling, elaborateness for earnestness, accuracy for emotion." Over twenty years later, this same reviewer looked back on Booth's entire career a few days after the actor's death. He saw it beginning in an attempt to dislodge the aging Edwin Forrest, thriving in a new climate of public refinement, and reaching a kind of perfection within the limits of its age.

> Mr. Booth's Hamlet ... met a new tradition of culture with the trademarks of culture. It suppressed passion and elaborated sentiment. It returned to the literary and poetic charms of the play with extraordinary gifts for their declaration, and in doing so it in a measure ignored the dramatic and tragic. Hamlet no longer shattered, it titillated. The divine bolts were left out, and in their place we got the steady but broken sensation of the Faradic current. Hamlet had become a nineteenth-century gentleman.
>
> It is just to acknowledge that Mr. Booth met and expressed a new condition of public taste. Whether that condition was only a reaction or was the normal and permanent development of intelligence may be an interesting subject of inquiry. My own opinion is that it marked an advance in matters of art in the direction of refinement.[26]

Crinkle goes on to relate this shift of taste in the theater to a larger shift in culture during the course of the century, in Europe as well as America. "This change had shown itself in literature already. We had seen it in the decline of Byron and the vogue of Tennyson, and we were to feel it more keenly in the eclipse of Victor Hugo by the pallid effulgence of George Eliot and Thomas Hardy."

Both Levine and this critic see the theater becoming attenuated, over-refined, and hence powerless, for audiences that grew more distant and fragmented, Levine's "group of mute [and individual] receptors." But what these discussions leave out of account is a different kind of active response that Booth in particular inspired. Instead of loudly signaling their im-mediate reactions, audiences did now sit quietly and attentively. But some individuals also responded deeply and long afterward. Some returned again and again until they knew Booth so well that they could repeat his words and gestures. A few actually disciplined themselves to record his perfor-mances in extensive notes.

The chief exhibit of this sort is a long record left by Charles W. Clarke, a young man who saw Booth so many times that he mastered *Hamlet* and could write it out from memory. Clarke was a twenty-one-year-old clerk in New York when he first went to see Booth in *Hamlet*. He had had a little literary success of his own by then; one of his stories had been published when he was seventeen. But he had not yet finished high school; he seems to have dropped out of school because of frail health and financial problems after the death of his father. The experience of seeing Booth was a sudden revelation to him of the full power of literature and drama. Clarke saw the performance on January 18. He was so overwhelmed by it that during his walk home he resolved to memorize the play and see Booth again as often as possible. Through hours of labor he committed the entire Cowden-Clarke edition to memory, pondered the way certain lines should be spoken, and read every scrap of criticism he could find. Then he went back to see Booth. He saw him altogether eight times — a feat in itself since Booth's careful delivery stretched a cut version of the play to four hours of playing time.

Out of all this study and observation, Clarke went on to compose his thorough record of how the actor moved and spoke in this part. Shattuck, an expert on Shakespearean theater history, estimates that the result is probably "the fullest record of any Shakespearean performance before the advent of the motion picture and the sound track" (*HEB*, p. 103). Through the following summer Clarke completed a fair copy of this work in over 200 columns of a two-column memorandum book. (His entries run from the column for April 29, 1870, through the column for November 10.) By then he was at his brother-in-law's farm near Rochester, New York.

He stayed there to finish school, and eventually married and moved west. He carried this book with him, but he went into business instead of literature. He died at the age of ninety-two in Spokane, Washington, in 1940, and his daughter found his book and donated it to the Folger Shakespeare Library in the 1950s.[27] Its contents are fully presented in Shattuck's reconstruction of the 1870 production; they record a powerful performance.[28]

The *Hamlet* that Clarke saw was not 'a complete text but a traditional cut version. Shattuck has traced its general features through the full extent of Booth's career (*HEB*, pp. xvi-xxiv). There was no Fortinbras story. There was no hint of bawdy or sexually suggestive language. Hamlet was emphatically the starring role, and Hamlet was a model of human dignity. His insults to the likes of Polonius and Osric were spoken in asides and soliloquies, out of their hearing. His coldness to Ophelia was, in Booth's view, a result of his inability ever to love her: his mother's actions had blasted his feelings for any woman; his was an intellectual rather than a passionate nature; and, in Booth's opinion, Ophelia was "the personification of pale and feeble-minded amiability" (*HEB*, p. 139). Hamlet's madness was entirely a matter of craft and cunning. And through this role Booth moved carefully, distinctly uttering each word to dispel rather than create mysteries or ambiguities. "If the theatre was a school, his performance was an illustrated lecture," Shattuck concludes. "If he intended to reduce his Hamlet-in-action to something like the good hero in contest with the bad villain . . . that was no obstacle to popular acceptance of what was popularly considered to be Shakespeare's most 'philosophical' play" (*HEB*, p. xxiv).

The traditional version, in other words, was developed by Booth to highlight Hamlet as a tortured but steadfast minister of justice. And Clarke's record shows just how he handled the burden of assassination. His execution of Claudius in the final scene was a searing culmination of his character throughout the play. The full details of the performance may or may not be accurately recorded in Clarke's formidable manuscript. But this point stands out distinctly.

On the whole, Booth's Hamlet is a prince of great gentleness, nobility, and intellect. "He is always the *prince*," Clarke writes; "and although his soul appears to be running a wild zig-zag course of self-reproach, philosophy, introspection, strong grief and overwrought imagination, he never falls into vulgar ways of exhibition in making these things known" (col. 75). But he is a prince with a deep streak of irresolution. He cannot square the nobility and consideration of his nature with the ever-clearer necessity of committing a deliberate murder. On small matters he is brilliant and decisive, but on the great issue of killing the king his will seems paralyzed. When he leaves Claudius unmolested at his prayers, Clarke sees him as "a man of first-class intellect but second-class will" (col. 129). And when he does kill Claudius (by rushing up and stabbing him through the neck — not, as in the uncut play, by forcing him to drink his own poison), he commits an act that leaves him overcome with horror. "Here, as elsewhere, Booth showed Hamlet's weakness when great responsibilities bore upon him. In a mood incited to desperation by the developments of Laertes he stabbed the King. It was clearly shown — the excitement of the fence, the heat by which he retorted wounds upon Laertes, and the additional heat that was cast into his inflamed state of mind when the Queen fainted and Laertes' resolutions were made — all these were indicated by an increased intensity of action" (col. 202). In other words, Hamlet had to be worked up by the surprising passions of the moment in order to do the deed.

Clarke's direct transcription shows this action in detail. Once Hamlet discovers that Laertes has conspired with the king to kill him, he "rises desperately with a furious face."

> Horatio sees his intention and catches his arm striving to stay him. Hamlet to avoid him runs along the front. Horatio keeps pace with him still between him and the King. Hamlet veers inward then suddenly throws off Horatio and darts toward the throne. The King is on the throne surrounded by guards and courtiers apparently making explanations and giving directions. There are cries of "Treason" and swords are drawn. A number oppose Hamlet. He sweeps down their weapons, and drives them aside; then bounds up the throne and seizes the King's throat in his left hand. With his right hand he plunges his foil through the King's neck twice.
>
> (cols. 198-99)

Here is the rush of energy Clarke saw, culminating in Hamlet's curse of Claudius: "Here, thou incestuous, murderous, damned Dane, follow my mother." But in pronouncing these words Hamlet's voice is almost "cramped." Clarke describes it as a "voice full of energy and mad exultation, cramped a little in utterance as if coming from overworking lungs or closed lips." From this point on Hamlet staggers with shock and horror.

Throws the King off, who falls backward from the throne amid those

below. Hamlet casts up his left hand with the fingers open and looks
after the King with a sudden start and stare of horror, then reels and
falters uncertainly down the steps of the throne with his left hand
upon his forehead. As he goes he drops his foil. Horatio receives him
in his arms at the rear centre.

(col. 199)

There is nowhere physically or spiritually for Hamlet to go beyond this
point. He can only die.

Clarke's further commentary insists that this is the final impression of
the play:

> But the instant that the King was killed, Booth's Hamlet shrank. His
> conscientiousness was outraged. His will was appalled for it had over-
> done itself and stepped beyond its sphere. And so Booth staggered
> from the deed as from some climax that was too high to be maintained.
> All his vigor departed. All his resolution vanished. His desperation
> dropped utterly away. He could not vindicate himself. He was too
> weak to assert the justice of his course by either bearing or words.
> So Booth went down from the throne in a bewildered way as one
> who is escaping from some danger, where the concussion is over but
> where the instinct of salvation which leads him to fly has not been
> counteracted by a consciousness of safety.
>
> (col. 202)

Clarke makes it clear that the collapse here is not a matter of Hamlet's
physical exhaustion or weakness due to the poison now working in his
veins. He collapses in spirit.

> There was no dignity—no sign that he would stand by his act and
> advocate its rightfulness. The deed was done—his purpose was ful-
> filled. That was all. There was that look upon his face which told
> that he would have been thankful and gratified if he was not aware
> that he had dallied weakly in the performance; but there was no
> strength left to brace himself against the criticism of the world and
> uphold the propriety of his work. . . . Had his will not been frustrate
> this same energy [that he used in checking Horatio from suicide]
> would have appeared in an effort to justify himself.
>
> (cols. 202-3)

Clarke concludes that Booth's Hamlet is thus forced to confront his own
weakness of will: "It seemed as if the experience of the hour by having
again exposed to him the faintness of his will, had thrown him back
upon his intellect and spirituality; whence looking about upon those

metaphysical fields where he was used to roam, the affairs of the present became puny in his eyes and he left them with indifference" (col. 203). Clarke admits that this is only one way of interpreting this scene: "this was one of the mental conditions that his acting suggested to me." But a later, general comment on the whole play seems to rule out another strong possibility here — that Hamlet is overwhelmed by remorse over what he has done. Booth's Hamlet, he writes, "is not distinctly conscientious. He fails to kill the king more through a lack of willpower, than through any excess of conscientious scruples. There are many places in Hamlet where Booth might show a shrinking from Hamlet's course caused by an un-willingness to do moral wrong or to slay a fellow creature: but in such places Booth depicts instead dearth of force in executing a foregone inten-tion" (col. 205).

But is it certain that conscience does not govern Hamlet's final scene? Clarke's evidence is not conclusive. This moment may just be too powerful to be reduced to any single interpretation. What Clarke actually saw was a sharp turn in Hamlet's behavior, from an energetic dash up the throne to a weak collapse back into Horatio's arms. He understands that final collapse as consistent with Hamlet's weakness and irresoluteness through-out the play. Yet it could just as well stand for a final turn in Hamlet's perception — if not a recoiling out of violated scruples, a recoiling from the exhaustion of a futile act. Claudius is slain, but the world has turned. Gertrude is dead. Laertes and Ophelia have been drawn after Polonius and Rosencrantz and Guildenstern, victims of Hamlet's implication in the long evil in Denmark. Now it is over. Claudius is dead; Hamlet knows himself to be dying. And as Clarke records the moment itself, the key terms are terms of moral judgment: "The instant that the king was killed, Booth's Hamlet shrank. His *conscientiousness* was outraged. His will was *appalled* for it had overdone itself and stepped beyond its sphere. . . . He could not *vindicate* himself. He was too weak to assert the *justice* of his course."

What exactly happened on stage is thus inadequately recorded. What it represented is even further clouded. What remains certain, however, is that here was an assassin onstage. Everyone knew it to be Booth as well as Hamlet. Here was the moment of climax after almost four hours of shared tension between the audience and this living legend of theatrical suffering and power. And once Hamlet did the deed, he perceptibly shrank. He collapsed in horror and died of his own poison, too.

Perhaps Clarke's record of the assassination in *Hamlet* is reinforced by the assassination scene in *Julius Caesar* as Booth produced it in 1871. The assassination was the central scene of that production, and as Brutus, Booth played a murderer who acted only when forced. According to a modern survey of *Caesar* stagings throughout history, this one made a new departure in stressing the reluctance of Brutus at this moment:

> It is worth noting that for the first time Brutus and Cassius are given characteristic and contrasting action as each confronts the Dictator at the scene's climax. Cassius, imperious and vicious, savours his conquest by pulling Caesar from the throne before he strikes him; then, lest Brutus weaken, he thrusts the dying figure at him. Brutus, on the contrary, has no stomach for violence. Trapped by Cassius' manoeuvre, he stabs with manifest reluctance and turns away in revulsion.
>
> (Ripley, p. 126)

Two other detailed accounts of Booth's *Hamlet* have also come to light to confirm Clarke's record. Both date from the 1880s and reflect later developments in the role, but they seem to show that the assassination scene remained consistent. In 1968 the Harvard Theatre Collection acquired a set of manuscripts by Mary Isabella Stone of Framingham, Massachusetts. These include an edition of *Hamlet* interleaved with over 200 pages of notes about Booth's performances in New York and Boston between 1879 and 1884. These notes show that Booth was aging (he turned fifty in 1883 and began to play Hamlet in a wig), but his interpretation of the role remained much the same. The assassination scene retained the same general action, though Stone believed Hamlet was overcome not by horror so much as by the rapid working of the poison through his body and his earnest concern to preserve the life of Horatio.[29] Another witness at about the same time was Hamlin Garland, then a young man eager to learn in Boston after years in Wisconsin, Iowa, and Dakota. For him, as for Clarke, Booth's performances were a revelation; they suddenly crystalized the meaning of all poetry and drama and left a lifelong impression. Garland, too, went back night after night; he, too, recorded Booth's work, in a series of lectures prepared in 1885 and delivered many times thereafter; he even submitted this work to Booth himself for comment and correction (*HEB*, pp. 302-5). Shattuck notes that Garland saw a very different Hamlet from Clarke's, an older, less elastic man, more settled in wisdom. He quotes Garland's descriptions of "the passive suffering center" of the action, "the good man enduring" (*HEB*, p. 304). But if the tone was somewhat different, the final deed remained much the same. Garland describes the assassination as a ritual of horror:

. . . Laertes gasps out his crime. With a wild cry Hamlet drops on his knees beside him, a look of ineffable horror and loathing on his face, then with his eyes flaming forth a desperate resolve he leaps upon the King and stabs him to the heart.

What horror is on his ghastly face and in his trembling limbs as he looks upon the works of his hands. As he stands tottering there, looking down upon the fallen King, it seems as though the endless unavailing remorse of the future rushed like a flood of fire through his brain.[30]

What may be most important about such records is not their details, but their combined witness to Booth's power as an actor. Clarke, Stone, and Garland all became devoted to him, quite independently. Each returned again and again to see him, studied his play, took notes, and then spent hundreds of laborious hours reconstructing his performances in a written record. This is an effect apparently unrivaled by any other actor in history. And in a curious way that power should make us wary about the accuracy of any detail in these records. What drove their authors to make them was an experience so deeply moving and mysterious that they had to expend enormous effort—actually had to reeducate themselves—in order to come to terms with it.

Such power had a price, of course, for the public as well as for Booth. There was a sense, voiced by some of his harsher critics, that Booth adapted himself to the effete, conservative taste of postwar elegant society in the urban North. He built his theater for fashionable New Yorkers, and enjoyed the company of millionaires and men of distinction of the kind that eventually became members of The Players. There was certainly a strain of longing in his career, for high-toned refinement, for dignity as an actor— a strain made all the deeper by his family history. To overcompensate, Booth had to make money. In the long run he succeeded in making the kind of income that went with private railway cars and a house on Gramercy Park. He lavished much of it on his theater and its debt. He spent freely and generously on others. He gave much away, thoughtfully and openhandedly. But he also enjoyed the comforts money could bring. No one could accuse him of being subtle or even sensible about financial matters. He probably was unaware of the extent to which he became a conservative New York capitalist and increased his own wealth at great cost to others. But by the late 1880s there were some who felt his tours had become sheer "money grabbing" devices, which exploited the sub-ordinate members of his cast, raked way the entire season's profits from stock companies in small communities, and served up shabby performances on an impossible schedule.[31] In retrospect it might seem, too, that he traded on some questionable capital — the notoriety, sympathy, sensationalism, or curiosity excited by the very name of Booth.

But the records of Clarke, Stone, and Garland show that he gave his audiences something precious of his very own. He died well loved for good reason. He was the last of his line, if not the last of the old-style tragedians, then the last of the virtuoso actors, whom theatergoers went to see again and again, and to measure against one another. And in a lifelong career he made himself the American Hamlet, the brooding, melancholy good man surviving in a dark time. "Pure, generous, high-minded, incapable of vulgar arts, either of defense or display, he lived upon the stage of the world, even as on the mimic stage, an ideal life." So he was memorialized soon after his death — with one further remark to clinch the point: "And the one appalling disaster and sorrow of his experience he bore with such patience and magnanimity as presently reconquered the favor of a shaken and bewildered nation. Only great men can thus greatly endure great griefs. The soul of Edwin Booth, like the art of Edwin Booth, was of the truly heroic type."[32] Edward H. Sothern put the matter more briefly and memorably: "Edwin Booth's genius shone like a good deed in a naughty world."[33] To paraphrase Samuel Johnson: in such lapidary inscriptions these authors were not under oath.

Yet despite his flaws, Booth endured through the deepest American grief of his time and shaped it into a noble reputation. He reached back across the footlights to impress tragic poetry on the hearts of thousands of individual playgoers. We know some were changed forever. Charles Clarke claimed he was restored from sickness to health, from lassitude to a new resolve to make something of himself, because of Booth's power as Hamlet. He followed through by crossing the continent to make a new life, carrying along his written record of that performance. More than a century later he and others still bear witness to Booth as a prince tortured and resolute under the burden of assassination, who night after night brought a revelation to its climax: political murder as a futile act, a hollow victory, a corrosive and self-destroying evil.

8

Ave atque Vale

*T*HE DEATH of Lincoln, like the death of Caesar, marks the end of one kind of government and the beginning of another. It dramatizes the difference by symbolizing it in the experience of one person rather than in the diffuse experiences of millions scattered over a vast empire. Caesar died by violence, and that was the end of Rome as a republic. Lincoln died by violence, and that was the end of the original American Constitution derived by consent and balanced argument in both North and South. Both events also dramatize the recognition that territorial expansion had outstripped the institutions of the founders. To go on as an empire, Rome came to require an emperor. To go on as a continental nation, America came to a constitutional crisis over slavery and freedom.

In the famous fourscore and seven years before Gettysburg, the geography of America had changed. Thirteen colonies along the Atlantic had come to be a solid block of twenty-nine states from the Atlantic to the far side of the Mississippi River, along with Kansas, Texas, Oregon, and California further west. The North and the South had become distinctive, separate regions, distrustful toward each other and self-sustaining in their widely different understandings of American government. What should have been the common framework holding them together could serve instead as a focus for contention. To the North, the Constitution could seem a guarantee of union and of eventual emancipation for all; to the South, it could seem a limited compact based on ongoing assent from sovereign states, and an explicit guarantee of slaveholders' rights to their property. These opposite, contentious understandings could only be worsened by further territorial expansion. Already the federal government had become large but remote. The presidency had been held not once but often by characters like Franklin Pierce and James Buchanan — not distinguished national figures like Washington, Jefferson, or Jackson, but obscure little men, talented chiefly at placid compromise. Meanwhile the pressure to settle the West had raised insoluble problems. Was the new land to be settled as slave-territory or free-territory; and which great older region was therefore to prevail in Congress and perhaps attain amending power over the Constitution?

The solution that emerged from the Civil War was a paradox that has continued to perplex generations of Americans. The election of 1860, secession, and the war brought these questions to a resolution by force. In the end the North won. By dint of its larger population and concentrated industrial and economic power, it went on for over a century as the dominant region, while the South was "reconstructed" and the West was settled and developed under a much-altered Constitution. But the North won under the presidency of the enigmatic Lincoln, a man who could accept and wield concentrated power but who also embodied the homely pioneer virtues, studiously mastered the high principles and high-flown rhetoric of the most libertarian founders, and imparted his own humble ideals to the common people. And at the precise point of victory Lincoln paid with his own life.

What endured about Lincoln was one shining fact: he freed the slaves. He not only freed them, but also took the first steps toward enfranchising them. And unlike other contemporary liberations, this emancipation did not merely affect a lower social order or a people indigenous to a far-flung colony. This was an outright acknowledgment of political equality for the most alien of the aliens who had settled in great numbers in America; for black-skinned people whose ancestors had come in chains and who themselves had been brought up as subhuman chattels — people with no expectations or education for citizenship, and with great social obstacles preventing their economic advancement, self respect, or concerted political action. It was certain after 1865 that there could not be another dissolution of the states. But it was just as certain that another great Father Abraham could never arise. And it would soon become clear that the proclamations of freedom made by white male northerners would have to be substantiated over a long period, by a geographical situation and a diversified citizenry still to be engendered.

Lincoln's era thus seems as far separate from the years that immediately followed it as it was from the glorious founding era to which he often turned. To see this point vividly, we need only consider a minor family dispute of John and Abigail Adams in 1776. While John was in Philadelphia in the Congress that declared independence, Abigail wrote him her famous lines about remembering the ladies. "Be more generous and favourable to them than your ancestors," she teased. "Remember all Men would be tyrants if they could. If particular care and attention is not paid to the Laidies we are determined to foment a Rebelion, and will not hold ourselves bound by any Laws in which we have no voice, or Representation." John Adams returned the kidding by insisting that women were already the real masters. "A fine Story indeed," he concluded. "I begin to think the Ministry [in England] as deep as they are wicked. After stirring up Tories, Landjobbers, Trimmers, Bigots, Canadians, Indians, Negroes, Hanoverians, Hessians, Russians, Irish Roman Catholicks, Scotch Renegadoes, at last they have stimulated the   to demand new Priviledges and threaten to rebell."[1] But the point stuck in John Adams's conscience, for a few weeks later he wrote another correspondent concerning voting rights for men who had no property. By the same reasoning that would justify that reform, he wrote, one could "prove that you ought to admit women and children; for, generally speaking, women and children have as good judgments, and as independent minds, as those men who are wholly destitute of property." The whole idea to Adams was "dangerous":

> Depend upon it, Sir, it is dangerous to open so fruitful a source of controversy and altercation as would be opened by attempting to alter the qualifications of voters; there will be no end of it. New claims will arise; women will demand a vote; lads from twelve to twenty-one will think their rights not enough attended to; and every man who has not a farthing, will demand an equal voice with any other, in all acts of state. It tends to confound all distinctions, and prostrate all ranks to one common level.[2]

To Adams, as to others of his generation, a franchise for propertyless black men was unimaginable. And Adams's prophecy has come to pass. New claims have arisen. The Constitution that was amended in 1870 to establish racial equality in voting was amended in 1920 to secure the vote for women and in 1971 to reduce the voting age to eighteen. The sweep of constitutional history after Lincoln has been precisely what Adams feared: "to confound all distinctions, and prostrate all ranks to one common level."

To look back to Lincoln, therefore, is to cross a barrier into another way of feeling and understanding the political world, even though Lincoln's own most vaunted claim seems to deny it. The creed of Gettysburg is that the ideals of the "fathers" of 1776 were being maintained, preserved, and defended, to be passed on to generations unborn. But in fact they were being transmuted beyond recognition. Not by Lincoln alone, not by the North rather than the South, but by a divided country caught in new circumstances that the founders had no way of foreseeing.

To look back at John Wilkes Booth in Ford's Theatre is likewise to regard him in terms that could not have been his own. His leap, his cry, his movement across the stage call up echoes and conventions that now have to be explained and recaptured. But with modern eyes we can also see dimensions beyond his imagining. His egalitarian, leveling shot from actor to president on Good Friday seems, after a century, not merely outrageous but strikingly fitting as the close of Lincoln's career. And his abrupt and violent intrusion into a padded domestic box also has its symbolic reverberations. He tore open the chamber of the Lincolns, just as the first massive and mechanized war had torn open the domestic security of thousands of American homes.

In short, the assassination of Lincoln belongs to another era — better said, it marks a division between eras. It seems as immediate in many ways as any historical event. It is the common knowledge of schoolchildren and adults. It touches directly what every American knows about the presidency, the Civil War, or nineteenth-century public life. But in fact it stands closer to John Adams and George Washington than to John F. Kennedy and Martin Luther King. It is a portal through which we can glimpse the old Constitution by the flash of a modern terrorist's pistol.

In a similar way, the assassination also marks the waning of tragedy. This is not simply because John Wilkes Booth was an actor. It is true that he crossed the barrier between the stage and the world, then leapt back to stain the stage with a martyr's blood. Many actors were arrested at the time, and Ford's Theatre was closed for good. But in fact the theater as a whole was able to withstand such an outrage. After a few months even Booth's brother could return and thrive as a tragedian, even in the roles of Hamlet and Brutus. It is rather that all the Booths played in a dying tradition. They, too, belonged to a world far removed from the conditions that followed the Civil War.

A common theater familiar to all theatergoers has never been geographically possible in America. The Booths traveled every year to play in city after city. Edwin kept traveling in what proved a vain attempt to establish one great theater in New York; but even if he had been successful in that enterprise, he would still have been established only there. As it was, he kept going on to engagements in Boston and Baltimore, Chicago and San Francisco, and appearing for a few nights each in many out-of-the-way auditoriums along his route. The enlargement of the country to continental dimensions made this work even harder. Junius Brutus Booth made just one trip to California—and died on the route home. Edwin began his career in California—and had to struggle to build and keep a name from coast to coast for the rest of his life.

The effect of old-fashioned tragedy depended on performances before cultivated audiences, city people who had seen other stars in the same roles and could draw detailed comparisons. In London this situation was commonplace. In New York it was frequent. In other cities it was just impossible. In many, the arrival of two stars in two seasons was a miraculous coincidence.

The events of the 1860s made these matters worse. Not only did the country move on to enormous westward expansion, it also went through experiences of grief and loss more vivid than anything on stage. The old suggestion that Booth killed Lincoln because he was a failing actor has this much tincture of truth. By April 1865, the names of Lincoln and Grant were not only filling the newspapers but they were also filling the seats of a theater for a Good Friday performance, far better than any actor could. Public prints were palpably more effective than theaters at addressing the entire nation and reflecting its common beliefs. And Lincoln's death was to provoke a public spectacle of unprecedented grandeur: a funeral train pageant from Washington to Springfield; parades, displays, and rituals in every major city; and silent homage and awe in fields and crossings all along the route. No such numbers had ever turned out for any event as they did now to personally witness the passing of Lincoln.

And after Lincoln was gone it became hard to imagine another tragic American hero. Lincoln himself grew to the stature of a nonpareil American martyr who was still in everyone's memory. Just as important, his principles eliminated the possibility of a successor. The idea of human equality, now ratified by war and explicitly embedded in the Constitution, ruled out—and still rules out—the inherent superiority of one person over another. It makes heroes a thing of the past, particularly tragic heroes who must assimilate and symbolize the identity of an entire people. Hereafter America would be too enormous and too emphatically democratic to be anything but uncontrollably pluralistic. Lincoln is not just the last, he is the only American political figure to fill the mind's eye. Only one room in the White House is still set apart with period furnishings—the Lincoln Bedroom.[3] It is inconceivable (indeed dreadful to consider) that another president could again have the focused power over a constitutional dilemma to earn a matching niche in history.

This change is not, of course, uniquely American. Tragedy has faded or reorganized itself in the past century for many reasons, including widespread democracy, pluralism, intercultural encounters around the world, and the mechanical transformation of the theater into films, videotapes, and simultaneous satellite broadcasts. Very recently, the rise of gender studies has posed hard questions about its remaining value. For the heroes of tragedy are mainly male: isolated, rational power wielders who destroy themselves and others in their unavoidable violations of rigid moral codes. Perhaps tragedy is an outworn or narrow form of art and civilization, better displaced by wider visions of human understanding, suffering, sharing, and growth.

Even so, the violence between Booth and Lincoln is still bound to figure in our memory of what tragedy has been. It cuts to the bone of American history. And in its recapitulation of the Brutus legend, it also cuts to the marrow of what Shakespeare imagined about the merging of tragedy and history. Shakespeare's high tragedies begin with *Julius Caesar* and *Hamlet*, but they conclude with further Roman plays and then yield to another way of seeing. It is misleading to say anything brief and firm about the course of Shakespeare's development. But *Antony and Cleopatra* answers *Julius Caesar* very directly with a wisdom far different from Hamlet's. That later play may touch our modern condition as pointedly as the earlier tragedies touched Booth's.

The close of *Antony and Cleopatra* resembles the ending of *Julius Caesar*. Again a noble Roman falls on his own sword when pursued to the east by the forces of Caesar. And here the long legend ends—with the death of Mark Antony and the final consolidation of imperial power by Octavian. But here the legend also takes another turn, for both Antony and Julius Caesar have been outlived by Cleopatra, and her dying is at once solemn and triumphant. She arranges to die richly as an inconquerable queen, mysterious and powerful in ways that no surviving Roman can comprehend.

Shakespeare knew well that such good Romans had long feared Cleopatra and hated her. To them she was an eastern sorceress who charmed and entangled and weakened their strongest men. She was a vile, dark-skinned "gypsy" out of barbaric Africa or the East. She was a ruthless adversary with ambitions of her own, to insinuate herself into Rome and seize its empire for herself. Shakespeare highlights all these dangers in her character, but she also becomes powerful on his stage as an inexhaustible source of erotic play and both earthy and unearthly grandeur. Antony and Enobarbus, who have experienced her magnificence, find it impossible to describe her to anyone who has not.

At the end of the play Cleopatra can scoff at the mere military and political power of Caesar. Her life, her love, her experiences of incomparable power and irrepressible loss have raised her far above him. She expresses a world-weary regard for this young Octavian who has taken her captive but can only be indifferent to her, intent as he is upon civic matters. At the opening of the final scene she accepts her own suicide as a greater deed than any he can accomplish:

> My desolation does begin to make
> A better life. 'Tis paltry to be Caesar;
> Not being Fortune, he's but Fortune's knave,
> A minister of her will. And it is great
> To do that thing that ends all other deeds,
> Which shackles accidents and bolts up change;
> Which sleeps, and never palates more the dung,
> The beggar's nurse and Caesar's.
>
> (5.2.1-8)

There is bravado in these lines, forced mockery against a power that is pushing Cleopatra toward self-destruction. But there is also a ring of truth. Octavian will become one of the greatest men in history; his defeat of Antony and Cleopatra makes him the sole emperor of the civilized world. But next to the wonder that these mighty lovers have known, he is a cold and "paltry" figure. As Cleopatra proves, he is driven on by a power outside himself as she is not. He must serve Rome, or in larger terms be a mere agent of a power like that of the gods. He has become the minister of Fortune—worse yet, the "knave" to do her dirty work. Cleopatra retains the dignity to let go of such ambition, to defy death and Fortune, to escape the mere material world where common "dung" feeds both emperor and beggar.

The splendor of her final moments cannot be fairly represented in this or any other single speech. But these lines may serve to show a defeat of Caesar quite different from assassination. Cleopatra speaks as a woman, an African, and an alien—precisely the kind of disenfranchised person who stood unassimilable outside the empire of early America as well as early Rome. But she claims a realm of her own, an immortal realm of the human spirit. And her American successors have laid claim to a more tangible place, in a modern open society. The Constitution that Lincoln left behind him is quite different from the one that brought him into office. In John Adams's words, modern American politics does indeed "tend to confound all distinctions, and prostrate all ranks to one common level." But the past two centuries have witnessed the strength of a nation growing not only geographically but socially and mentally to admit all conceivable candidates for citizenship and respect.

What is more, Cleopatra's words link this modern condition to important moments in the past. They thus hold out some assurance that realized democracy need not be a flickering and transient development of our time. "'Tis paltry to be Caesar" may be Shakespeare's judgment as well as Cleopatra's. It is a line that nicely closes the sequence of his tragedies from *Julius Caesar* to *Antony and Cleopatra*. For that matter, it nicely closes his many years of dramatizing kings and heroes who often proved just as frail, limited, or vain as dozens of his other men and women. The line might well echo Shakespeare's awareness that he had created his own Caesars on stage and served royal audiences through a long career, and seen around both. His imagination held other possibilities of human life and would go on making poetry after the fall of any mortal, however mighty. And beyond Shakespeare's art lay the actual stories of Rome— the fall of one Caesar at the hand of Brutus and the rise of another through the destruction of Antony and Cleopatra. Rome as an ideal empire held its Caesars to its own unforgiving standards of piety, republicanism, and law. The death of Cleopatra by her own hand, like the deaths of Antony, Brutus, and Cato, is a Roman gesture of protest against power concentrated by a tyrant. "'Tis paltry to be Caesar," is Cleopatra's stinging taunt, but she speaks for a long history. We might dare hope that this line is more enduring and effective than its rival, "Sic semper tyrannis."

There is one further measure of the events of 1865 that carries the weight of long history. It is a poem from the ancient world, written around

the time of Caesar's assassination. Catullus's lines at his brother's tomb
nicely frame the strange and touching relationship that developed between
Edwin and John Wilkes Booth. In 57 B.C., Catullus traveled to the east
and made a visit to the tomb of his brother, who had died in the area
near ancient Troy. His poem 101 has endured over 2,000 years as an almost
untranslatable elegy. Its first six lines sum up the situation of the poet's
arduous travel to visit this spot just once; the remainder of the poem is
a very formal expression of grief. Here is the Latin text along with a close
prose translation:

> Mvltas per gentes et multa per aequora vectus
>   advenio has miseras, frater, ad inferias,
> ut te postremo donarem munere mortis
>   et mutam nequiquam alloquerer cinerem,
> quandoquidem fortuna mihi tete abstulit ipsum,
>   heu miser indigne frater adempte mihi.
> nunc tamen interea haec, prisco quae more parentum
>   tradita sunt tristi munere ad inferias,
> accipe fraterno multum manantia fletu,
>   atque in perpetuum, frater, ave atque vale.[4]

Borne through many lands and over many seas I have come, brother,
to this final rite of grief, to give you the last offerings for the dead
and to speak in vain to your silent ashes, since fate has taken you
yourself away from me—oh, brother, how wrongly bereft me of you!
Now, anyhow, these gifts which by old custom of family are handed
on as a sad offering in funeral: take them wet with your brother's
many tears and forever, brother, hail and farewell.

Part of what makes this poem hard to translate is the intricate ease and
formality of the final lines. We cannot say "hail and farewell" or anything
comparable without stumbling over awkward language or stiff formality.
Latin has "ave" and "vale," simple words, very much alike in sound.
Catullus joins them here in a phrase—"ave atque vale"—that blurs three
similar a/e vowel patterns together. Hail is almost identified with farewell
here: the approach and the departure are superimposed on one another.
And with "frater" the pattern deepens. Brother greets brother at the same
time that a living man, busy traveling in the bright world of many lands
and seas, takes leave of this tomb forever.

It may seem odd to claim that this poem fits the relation of Edwin to
John Wilkes Booth, for Edwin did not visit his brother's grave or publicly

honor his memory. He agreed with the government to raise no special marker in the family plot in Baltimore, and he destroyed, suppressed, or recoiled from almost every reminder of the assassin. Yet we have also seen that this brother remained close to Edwin's life and work. Traveling through many lands and over many seas, Edwin approached his brother's life and death every time he performed *Hamlet*. He passed on the family heritage of Shakespearean tragedy as he reenacted the futility of the assassin's deed.

Woven through this short poem are some of the most essential feelings of tragedy, condensed into elegy. These simultaneous feelings of attraction and repulsion correspond to Aristotle's categories of pity and fear. Here they are raised to a pleasurable experience by Catullus's evident mastery of word and phrase and pattern. And these feelings retain their grandeur even in these few lines. The poet has been attracted enough to make a voyage to a distant land, and yet his separation from his brother is insuperable, his parting is "in perpetuum," forever. The poem thus insists that struggles of brother with brother both do and do not end. The fallen brother keeps his silence, while the survivor must find some means of expression in order to go on with an identity that is both continuous — a matter of ongoing custom and family — and wholly new, a determined effort on this side of a wall of grief.

To readers of the present century, this poem may also frame the history of Lincoln along with the Booths. The apostrophe from brother to brother, comrade to comrade, stands out as an ancient but distanced gesture — from an era when America was still an outpost of European culture: masculine, literate, steeped in republican Roman slogans still half-remembered from the late eighteenth century. To look back at Lincoln we, too, must sense an impossible barrier of time and change at the same moment that we recognize features as familiar as any we have known from childhood and its pennies. We, too, must say "vale" as well as "ave" to that haunting bearded face.

And beyond Lincoln, in the worlds of Shakespeare, and of Caesar's Rome, and even of the plains of Troy where Catullus's brother had his grave, we can almost feel the pull of honorable masculine warfare and respect. They seem to claim our patriotic recollection and yet lie forever beyond our approach. In a time of mechanized intercontinental warfare — of civilians, by civilians, and against civilians — old warriors of sword and pistol exert a romantic appeal. In a time of irresolvable conflicts and factions, of streets, highways, and airwaves humming with the noises of polyglot controversy, it is easy to long for the clarity of first principles in high and indelible phrases. But Booth's assault upon Lincoln is the point where these possibilities clearly end. Politics, poetry, and theater all converge there more tellingly than any of the principals ever knew.

Notes

Chapter 2: Brutus

1. *Shakespeare's Plutarch*, ed. T. J. B. Spencer (Harmondsworth, Eng.: Penguin, 1964), pp. 92-95; hereafter cited as Spencer. I have silently altered Spencer's punctuation and arrangement of speeches on the page.

2. Gaius Suetonius Tranquillus, *The Lives of the Caesars*, 1.82, in *Suetonius*, trans. J. C. Rolfe, 2 vols., The Loeb Classical Library (London: Heinemann; Cambridge, Mass.: Harvard University Press, 1930), 1: 111.

3. *Julius Caesar*, 2.1.292-302. I quote from *The Riverside Shakespeare*, ed. G. Blakemore Evans (Boston: Houghton Mifflin, 1974).

4. Hans Baron, *The Crisis of the Early Italian Renaissance*, rev. 1-vol. ed. (Princeton: Princeton University Press, 1966), pp. 48-54.

5. *Gulliver's Travels*, bk. 3, chap. 7. I quote from Jonathan Swift, *Gulliver's Travels and Other Writings*, ed. Louis A. Landa (Boston: Houghton Mifflin, 1960), p. 159.

6. Ronald Syme, *The Roman Revolution* (Oxford: Clarendon Press, 1939), p. 59.

7. Stefan Weinstock, *Divus Julius* (Oxford: Clarendon Press, 1971), p. 411.

8. William Shakespeare, *Julius Caesar*, ed. Arthur Humphreys (Oxford: Clarendon Press, 1984), pp. 10-24.

9. The opening scene, for example, shows the tribunes Flavius and Murellus agreeing to "disrobe the images" (1.1.64). It is impossible to know immediately from the text that this refers to diadems or festoons placed on images or statues of Caesar. Yet the audience is expected to notice this touch because later Casca mentions it: "Murellus and Flavius, for pulling scarves off Caesar's images, are

put to silence" (1.2.285-86). And of course this silencing is a telling act of Caesar's oppression: his chastening of the untouchable tribunes.

10. D. A. Russell, *Plutarch* (London: Duckworth, 1972), p. 101.

11. I quote from North's translation in Roland Baughman's modern spelling edition, *The Lives of the Noble Grecians and Romans*, 2 vols. (New York: Heritage Press, n.d.), 2: 1775.

Chapter 3: Shakespeare's Tragic Tyrannicides

1. *Johnson on Shakespeare*, ed. Arthur Sherbo, Yale Edition of the Works of Samuel Johnson, 7 (New Haven: Yale University Press, 1968), 74.

2. I quote from *The Riverside Shakespeare*, ed. G. Blakemore Evans (Boston: Houghton Mifflin, 1974).

Chapter 4: Brother against Brother

1. Edwin Booth to Nahum Capen, July 28, 1881, in Edwina Booth Grossman, *Edwin Booth: Recollections by His Daughter* (1894; rpt. New York: Benjamin Blom, 1969), pp. 227-28.

2. Garrie Davidson's account of helping destroy these effects is reported in Otis Skinner, *Footlights and Spotlights* (Indianapolis: Bobbs-Merrill, 1924), pp. 178-84.

3. Quoted in Francis Wilson, *John Wilkes Booth: Fact and Fiction of Lincoln's Assassination* (Boston: Houghton Mifflin, 1929), p. 234.

4. *UB*. The original manuscripts for this work were bequeathed to the Farjeon family and are now in a private collection in England. They were brought to Maryland by the actor Arthur Kincaid and exhibited during a conference on John Wilkes Booth in May 1988.

5. The various conspiracy theories that have arisen to explain Booth's act are thoroughly reviewed in William Hanchett, *The Lincoln Murder Conspiracies* (Urbana: University of Illinois Press, 1983). Booth's sanity, as well as the purposeful sanity of many other assassins, has been cogently defended in James W. Clarke, *American Assassins: The Darker Side of Politics* (Princeton: Princeton University Press, 1982), pp. 18-39.

6. "Editor's Easy Chair," *Harper's New Monthly Magazine*, 28 (December 1863), 131-33.

7. Lawrence W. Levine, *Highbrow/Lowbrow: The Emergence of Cultural Hierarchy in America* (Cambridge, Mass.: Harvard University Press, 1988), pp. 57-59. Levine takes this report very literally, as though the editor of *Harper's* had taken an actual rustic visitor around New York on a certain night. The essay device of such a tour is, however, at least as old as early-eighteenth-century journalism. Mr. Spectator tours London in this way with Sir Roger de Coverly!

8. Gordon Samples, *Lust for Fame: The Stage Career of John Wilkes Booth* (Jefferson, N.C.: McFarland, 1982), pp. 196-224. This list is too full to be completely trusted; it includes, for example, a performance in Boston within hours of a peformance in Richmond (p. 207).

9. Stanley Kimmel, *The Mad Booths of Maryland*, 2d ed. (New York: Dover, 1969), pp. 168, 262-63. The quotation is from the Boston *Daily Advertiser*, May 19, 1862; see Samples, pp. 88-89.

10. Eleanor Ruggles, *Prince of Players: Edwin Booth* (New York: Norton, 1953), p. 122.

11. John Cannon, ed., *The Letters of Junius* (Oxford: Clarendon Press, 1978), p. xix.

12. Leslie Stephen, *History of English Thought in the Eighteenth Century*, 2 vols. (1876; rpt. New York: Harbinger, 1962), 2: 170.

13. Joseph Smithers, *The Life of Joseph Addison*, 2d ed. (Oxford: Clarendon Press, 1968), p. 265; Colley Cibber, *An Apology for the Life of Colley Cibber*, ed. B. R. S. Fone (Ann Arbor: University of Michigan Press, 1968), pp. 251-52.

14. William Winter, *The Life and Art of Edwin Booth*, 2d ed. (1894; rpt. New York: Benjamin Blom, 1972), p. 397. See the Booth family tree outlined in Kimmel, following p. 38.

15. Spencer, p. 110. I have silently emended punctuation of internal quotations.

16. Ex parte Merryman, 17 Federal Cases, 144 (1861), rpt. in *Documents of American History*, ed. Henry Steele Commager, 9th ed. (New York: Appleton-Century-Crofts, 1973), 1: 400; hereafter cited as Commager.

17. Message to Congress in Special Session, July 4, 1861, in *LCW*, 4: 430. In fact Lincoln appears to have heeded Taney's decision in this case; Merryman was soon released from Fort McHenry, charged in a federal circuit court, and eventually freed. See J. G. Randall, *Constitutional Problems under Lincoln*, rev. ed. (Urbana: University of Illinois Press, 1951), p. 162n.

18. Don E. Fehrenbacher, *Lincoln in Text and Context: Collected Essays* (Stanford: Stanford University Press, 1987), pp. 123-24.

19. Matthew Page Andrews, "James Ryder Randall," in *The Library of Southern Literature*, ed. Edward Anderson Alderman and Joel Chandler Harris, 16 vols. (Atlanta: Martin and Hoyt, 1907-13), 10: 4313. See also the entry on Randall in the *Dictionary of American Biography*.

20. The original cover and the words of three northern versions are reproduced in Vera Brodsky Lawrence, *Music for Patriots, Politicians, and Presidents* (New York: Macmillan, 1975), pp. 360-61.

21. I quote stanzas 1, 2, and 5 from *The Library of Southern Literature*, 10: 4318-19.

22. A recent book attempts to link Booth's plots, actions, and escape to a well-planned and coordinated Confederate scheme for abducting Lincoln early in 1865, a scheme in which Booth was a pivotal agent. But the authors admit that all their evidence is and must be circumstantial, because even an enormous scheme of this sort had to operate covertly and leave no traces of evidence behind. See William A. Tidwell with James O. Hall and David Winfred Gaddy, *Come Retribution: The Confederate Secret Service and the Assassination of Lincoln* (Jackson: University of Mississippi Press, 1988).

23. Well-documented surveys of these sentiments include J. G. Randall, "The Unpopular Mr. Lincoln," in *Lincoln: The Liberal Statesman* (New York: Dodd,

Mead, 1947), pp. 65-87; David Donald, *Lincoln Reconsidered* (New York: Knopf, 1956), pp. 3-6; and Hanchett, pp. 7-34.

Chapter 5: The Tragic Lincoln

1. Don E. Fehrenbacher, *Lincoln in Text and Context: Collected Essays* (Stanford: Stanford University Press, 1987), p. 163.

2. Ibid., pp. 176-77. The New York *Herald* quotation is dated Sept. 17, 1865. The line "taking him for all in all," of course, recalls Hamlet's sorrowing lines about his father in Act 1: "He was a man, take him for all in all, / I shall not look upon his like again."

3. See also the fuller account of this episode in Roy P. Basler, *A Touchstone for Greatness* (Westport, Conn.: Greenwood Press, 1973), pp. 207-17.

4. Tyler Dennett, ed., *Lincoln and the Civil War in the Diaries and Letters of John Hay* (1939; rpt. New York: Da Capo, 1988), p. 188; see also Stanley Kimmel, *The Mad Booths of Maryland*, 2d ed. (New York: Dover, 1969), pp. 392-93.

5. The Marquis de Chambrun, "Personal Recollections of Mr. Lincoln," *Scribner's Magazine*, 13 (1893), 34-35.

6. Such memoirs are collected in Robert N. Reeves, "Abraham Lincoln's Knowledge of Shakespeare," *Overland Monthly*, ser. 2, 43 (1904), 336-42; Basler, *Touchstone for Greatness*, pp. 217-27.

7. David Donald, *Charles Sumner and the Rights of Man* (New York: Knopf, 1970), p. 214.

8. Edward L. Pierce, *Memoir and Letters of Charles Sumner*, 4 (Boston: Roberts Brothers, 1893), 233. The anecdote originally appeared in *The Works of Charles Sumner* (Boston: Lee and Shephard, 1874), 9: 360.

9. David Donald, ed., *Inside Lincoln's Cabinet: The Civil War Diaries of Salmon P. Chase* (New York and London: Longmans, Green, 1954), p. 149 (Sept. 22, 1863). The cartoon is reprinted and discussed in Rufus Rockwell Wilson, *Lincoln in Caricature* (New York: Horizon Press, 1953), p. 100, pp. 200-201. For extensive discussion of Lincoln as a canny but sometimes out-of-place storyteller, see the first three essays in Gabor S. Boritt, ed., *The Historian's Lincoln* (Urbana: University of Illinois Press, 1988), pp. 3-29.

10. Thomas J. Pressly, *Americans Interpret Their Civil War* (1953; rpt. New York: Free Press, 1965), esp. pp. 25-77.

11. Lincoln to William H. Herndon, Feb. 2, 1848, in *LCW*, 1: 448.

12. Edmund Wilson, *Patriotic Gore* (New York: Oxford University Press, 1962), p. 437.

13. 2 vols. (Philadelphia: National Publishing Co.; Chicago: Ziegler, McCurdy, 1868-70).

14. Stephens was not directly named for Alexander Hamilton; he adopted his middle name from a well-loved teacher in his youth, Alexander Hamilton Webster. See Rudolph Von Abele, *Alexander H. Stephens* (1946; rpt. Westport, Conn.: Negro Universities Press, 1971), p. 33.

15. Quoted from an 1805 letter to the Indiana Territorial Legislature, in Gerald

Stourzh, *Alexander Hamilton and the Idea of Republican Government* (Stanford: Stanford University Press, 1970), p. 190.

16. I have traced this relationship in two earlier studies, *The Authority of Publius* (Ithaca, N.Y.: Cornell University Press, 1984), and *American Silhouettes* (New Haven: Yale University Press, 1987), esp. pp. 85-114.

17. Lord Charnwood, *Abraham Lincoln* (New York: Holt, 1916), p. vi.

18. *LCW*, 5: 537. The italics and punctuation here are from Lincoln's signed draft.

19. This is the large point developed in Henry V. Jaffa's thorough study of the issues behind the Lincoln-Douglas debates: *Crisis of the House Divided* (1959; rpt. Chicago: University of Chicago Press, 1982).

Chapter 6: John Wilkes Booth as Brutus

1. "To Thomas Hume, Esq., M.D.," in *The Poetical Works of Thomas Moore*, ed. A. D. Godley (London: Oxford University Press, 1910), pp. 116-17. *Davi* is the plural of Davos, a common name for a Roman slave.

2. Noah Brooks, *Washington, D.C., in Lincoln's Time*, ed. Herbert Mitgang (New York: Collier Books, 1962), p. 271.

3. William Hanchett, *The Lincoln Murder Conspiracies* (Urbana: University of Illinois Press, 1983), p. 134. The title page of the song version is reproduced in Stanley Kimmel, *The Mad Booths of Maryland*, 2d ed. (New York: Dover, 1969), p. 214.

4. I quote from the version titled "Give Him a Sepulchre," printed in *UB*, pp. 145-47. This version bears the following headnote: " 'In memory of one who is said to have been buried in the ocean, that his grave might not be identified.' — By Gen. Tyrrel, Texas. Sent to Mrs. J. B. Booth [i.e., Booth's mother] by the writer." On its way back to Washington, Booth's body was rowed out onto the Potomac, and the impression was given that it was unceremoniously dumped there. A sketch of this purported burial at sea appeared on the front page of *Frank Leslie's Illustrated Newspaper* for May 20, 1865, reprinted as the frontispiece to George S. Bryan, *The Great American Myth* (New York: Carrick and Evans, 1940).

5. New York *Herald* report, quoted in Lloyd Lewis, *Myths after Lincoln* (New York: Harcourt, Brace, 1929), p. 122. *Frank Leslie's Illustrated Newpaper* for May 6, 1865, also mentioned a "discoloration . . . around the eyes" when Lincoln lay in state at the White House (p. 103), but the Washington *National Intelligencer* for April 19 reported: "The face and features look quite natural, and much credit is due to the embalmer" (p. 2, col. 4). Since embalmers traveled with the body, it is hard to believe that they worked to keep it looking purposely hideous. It is important to recall that embalming was unusual before the Civil War and did not become a widespread practice until late in the century. The pageant of displaying Lincoln's body in city after city was in itself a dramatic reminder of the way many soldiers had recently been embalmed and shipped home from battle for proper burial.

6. Charles Mason's diary for April 23, 1865, 43: 7, transcribed in Charles

Mason Remey, ed., "Life and Letters of Judge Charles Mason of Iowa: Middle Western Pioneer, 1804-1882" (typescript made in Washington, D.C., 1932), vol. 6, chap. 19. I have consulted the Columbia University copy.

7. Here and in what follows I quote from the transcription in Bryan, *The Great American Myth*, pp. 302-3, with minor emendations where such changes are indicated by two other transcriptions. The diary itself was written in pencil which has now faded. A line-by-line transcription was prepared by Frank Hebblethwaite of Ford's Theatre National Historical Site in September 1983; and a transcription prepared from enlarged photographs made by the F.B.I. appears in William B. Hanchett, "Booth's Diary," *Journal of the Illinois State Historical Society*, 72, no. 1 (Feb. 1979), 40-43.

8. Rufus Rockwell Wilson, *Lincoln in Caricature* (New York: Horizon Press, 1953), pp. xii-xiii, 324-25.

9. Tom Taylor, *Our American Cousin*, printed from "an acting text that includes Sothern's additions," in *British Plays of the Nineteenth Century*, ed. J. O. Bailey (New York: Odyssey Press, 1966), p. 207. See also Clara E. Laughlin, *The Death of Lincoln* (New York: Doubleday, Page, 1909), pp. 270-82.

10. Laughlin, p. 293; play quotation from Taylor, p. 215.

11. Gordon Samples, *Lust for Fame: The Stage Career of John Wilkes Booth* (Jefferson, N.C.: McFarland, 1982), p. 16 and n.

12. See Bryan, pp. 159-61, who cites several sources.

13. *UB*, p. 139; Hanchett, *Conspiracies*, p. 37.

14. All these details are recounted by careful historians of the assassination such as Hanchett, Kimmel, and Bryan. But the fact that Booth entrusted his letter to Matthews has an odd character that they do not notice. In Taylor's play Matthews had the role of a wicked legal agent who holds an old mortgage on the family estate. The mortgage was actually canceled long ago, but this agent keeps the release locked away in his special cabinet. In short, the plot turns on his holding this secret document, just as in real life the actor who played this role was carrying Booth's secret message which could unravel the meaning of the assassination. In the play, the wicked agent's name is Coyle. The editor of the *National Intelligencer* also happened to be named John F. Coyle. Maybe Booth enjoyed a neat little joke when he came upon Matthews and gave him his letter, thus sending his special manifesto to Coyle by way of "Coyle." But I stop here and leave to other ingenious investigators the task of piecing such clues into yet another assassination theory.

15. Quoted in W. Edwin Hemphill, "The Symbolism of Our Seal," *Virginia Cavalcade*, 2, no. 3 (Winter 1952), 27. A discussion of the long history of engravings of this seal appears in Edward S. Evans, *The Seals of Virginia*, published as part of the report of the Virginia State Library for 1909-10 (Richmond: Superintendent of Public Printing, 1911), esp. pp. 31-44. Evans also describes a design suggested at the time by Benjamin Franklin, portraying a similar idea but with different figures (p. 32):

Moses — standing on the shore and extending his hand over the sea, thereby causing the same to overwhelm Pharoah, who is sitting in an open chariot, a crown on his head, and a sword in his hand. Rays from a pillow [pillar?] of fire in the clouds, reaching to Moses, to express that he acts by command of the Deity.

Motto — Rebellion to Tyrants, in [is?] obedience to God.

In August 1776 Franklin proposed almost the same design for the Great Seal of the United States. See *The Papers of Benjamin Franklin*, vol. 22, ed. William B. Wilcox (New Haven: Yale University Press, 1982), pp. 562-63. I have used this source to suggest the bracketed corrections in the above quotation. This volume of the Franklin *Papers* also prints this motto as part of an epitaph to the regicide John Bradshaw, a widely printed epitaph and motto, which Franklin probably invented as a hoax (pp. 303-4).

16. Bryan, p. 182. Kimmel (p. 357) cites a newspaper clipping of 1878 that debunks Stewart as a "fraud"; it claims that with his gigantic, healthy stride he would surely have caught Booth if he really had gone after him.

17. Bryan, p. 302, emended as explained above in note 7. There may be a recollection of *Hamlet* here. When Booth wrote, "God simply made me the instrument of his punishment," he may (as an actor and child of an acting family) have recalled Hamlet's reflection after the murder of Polonius:

> For this same lord,
> I do repent; but heaven hath pleas'd it so
> To punish me with this, and this with me
> That I must be their scourge and minister.
> I will bestow him, and will answer well
> The death I gave him.
>
> (3.4.172-77)

An influential interpretation of Hamlet as God's appointed instrument of punishment takes these as the crucial lines of the play: Fredson Bowers, "Hamlet as Minister and Scourge," *PMLA*, 70 (1955), 740-49.

18. *Hamlet*, 3.3.36-43, 48-54; I quote from *The Riverside Shakespeare*, ed. G. Blakemore Evans (Boston: Houghton Mifflin, 1974). It was this soliloquy that Lincoln singled out for praise in his letter to James Hackett in 1863.

19. Hanchett, *Conspiracies*, p. 256. The letter to Booth's mother is reproduced and transcribed in *The Lincoln Log*, 2, no. 4 (May/June 1977), 1-3.

20. Bryan, pp. 240-43. See also Kimmel, pp. 396-98, and reproductions of Booth's holograph (in part) in the *Lincoln Log* issue just cited, pp. 4-5.

21. Booth prepared a longer draft of an address on the issues of the war, just after South Carolina became the first state to secede in 1860. It consists of fourteen manuscript pages, plus many further passages marked for insertion. It was never finished and never published; the draft is now preserved at the Hampden-Booth Theatre Library at The Players in New York City. See the description in Hanchett, *Conspiracies*, pp. 39-40, and a brief article with a few quotations: Jeannine Clark Dodels, "John Wilkes Booth's Secession Crisis Speech of 1860," in Arthur Kincaid, ed., *John Wilkes Booth, Actor*, proceedings of a conference in Bel Air, Md., May 1988 (privately printed, 1989), pp. 48-51.

22. "Death of Abraham Lincoln: Lecture deliver'd in New York, April 14, 1879 — in Philadelphia, '80 — in Boston, '81," in Walt Whitman, *Prose Works 1892, Vol. 2: Collect and Other Prose*, ed. Floyd Stovall, *The Collected Writings of Walt Whitman* (New York: New York University Press, 1964), 505. Whitman is of course mistaken on a couple of matters: Booth leapt about ten feet and broke his leg.

23. Whitman, p. 508. "Personalism" is a word Whitman coined to describe the personal individuality that could unfold in a democracy. He explores the idea in the central part of *Democratic Vistas* (1871).

24. This moral was, in fact, drawn very quickly. In his diary for April 16, 1865, Charles Mason wrote his impressions on hearing of the attacks of Lincoln and Seward, both of which were assumed to be fatal:

> I cannot but feel that at all events retributive justice has been raising her avenging hand against the two authors of the "impossible [irrepressible?] conflict" doctrine which has steeped the country in blood and overwhelmed it with woe. Lincoln and Seward were the apostles of that gospel. They might, either of them, have prevented the Civil War. They would not do it. "He who could forbid, he who should forbid, and yet does not forbid, commands." I therefore regard these men as responsible for the war. Although others were culpa[ble] that culpability does not exonerate these delinquents. How many of them have been punished, each in his own way. This double assassination may be justly regarded as the legitimate offspring of our Civil War. The instinctive shudder with which we contemplate the wounds or death of a fellow being having been deadened by custom or even by hearing of bloodshed and murder, men are more than half prepared for any murderous atrocity. Had it not been for this war neither Mr. Lincoln nor Mr. Seward would have been in any danger of assassination. They who countenanced the resort to the sword have felt its edge. This is thrown out as a mere philosophic reflection and not by way of apology or justification.

Charles Mason diaries, 43: 6-7, from the typescript cited above in note 6.

Chapter 7: Edwin Booth as Hamlet

1. Quoted in Richard Lockridge, *Darling of Misfortune: Edwin Booth* (1932; rpt. New York: Benjamin Blom, 1971), pp. 168-69. Lockridge notes that the *Herald* was especially hard on William Stuart, the Irish-born manager of the Winter Garden. Other managers refused to advertise in the *Herald* because it frequently attacked the immorality of the modern stage; but Stuart went a step further. He ran advertisements elsewhere that read, "This Establishment Does Not Advertise in the *New York Herald*" (Lockridge, pp. 166-67).

2. Press descriptions of several ovations are summarized in *HEB*, p. 62.

3. This incident was confirmed and explained by Robert Lincoln in "Edwin Booth and Lincoln," *Century Magazine*, 77 (1909), 919-20; the same article contains Edwin's letter to Adam Badeau, written April 16, 1865, expressing his first shocked feeling at news of the assassination.

4. Stanley Kimmel states that Edwin paid for rebuilding the barn, in *The Mad Booths of Maryland*, 2d ed. (New York: Dover, 1969), p. 364, n. 57. But published letters from Booth to the Garretts mention only a gift of books. See Betsy Fleet, ed., "A Chapter of Unwritten History: Richard Baynham Garrett's Account of the Flight and Death of John Wilkes Booth," *Virginia Magazine of History and Biography*, 71 (1963), 387-407, esp. 404-7.

5. See his letters to William Winter from Louisville, March 14, 1876; from Boston, Dec. 6, 1881; and from Paris, May 1, 1883, in *Between Actor and Critic: Selected Letters of Edwin Booth and William Winter*, ed. Daniel J. Watermeier (Princeton: Princeton University Press, 1971), pp. 58-59, 198, 246.

6. Eleanor Ruggles, *Prince of Players: Edwin Booth* (New York: Norton, 1953), pp. 253, 386. Asia Booth Clarke expresses the family's feeling that Corbett saved them from the agony of a long trial and a hanging: "We regard Boston Corbett as our deliverer, for by his shot he saved our beloved brother from an ignominious death." See Clarke, *The Unlocked Booth* (1938; rpt. New York: Arno, 1977), p. 140.

7. Booth received reassuring telegrams from her doctor before Mary suddenly developed alarming symptoms of pneumonia (*HEB*, pp. 48-49).

8. Asia Booth Clarke, *The Elder and the Younger Booth* (Boston: Osgood, 1882), pp. 174-75; hereafter cited as *EYB*. Watermeier states that Booth's debt to his father-in-law was over $200,000 (*Between Actor and Critic*, p. 83).

9. New York *Evening Post*, March 16, 1870, quoted in *HEB*, p. xiii.

10. Quoted in *HEB*, p. 90.

11. San Francisco *Daily Placer Times and Transcript*, April 29, 1853, quoted in *HEB*, pp. 6-7. Ewer's two essays on Booth's early Hamlet are also quoted and discussed more fully in Charles H. Shattuck, "Edwin Booth's First Critic," *Theatre Survey*, 7 (1966), 1-14.

12. Horace Traubel, *With Walt Whitman in Camden, I (March 28-July 14, 1888)* (1905; rpt. New York: Rowman and Littlefield, 1961), p. 355.

13. "The Old Bowery: A Reminiscence of New York Plays and Acting Fifty Years Ago," in Walt Whitman, *Prose Works 1892: Collect and Other Prose*, ed. Floyd Stovall (New York: New York University Press, 1964), pp. 595-96. This essay was originally published as "Booth and 'The Bowery' " in 1885.

14. Quoted in Lockridge, p. 80. Compare William Winter's critique of Oct. 4, 1862, quoted in *HEB*, p. 48: "From first to last, he not only does not make points where points are usually made, but he does not make a point at all."

15. *HEB*, pp. 18-30; Adam Badeau, "Edwin Booth On and Off the Stage: Personal Recollections," *McClure's Magazine*, 1 (Aug., 1893), 255-67.

16. Jefferson's memorial speech at The Players a year after Booth's death, reprinted in Francis Wilson, *Joseph Jefferson* (London: Chapman and Hall, 1906), pp. 143-48.

17. To Edwin Booth, July 17, 1859, in L. Terry Oggel, ed., *The Letters and Notebooks of Mary Devlin Booth* (Westport, Conn.: Greenwood Press, 1987), p. 5. Oggel's careful transcription of these letters has corrected and helped preserve the full record of this marital collaboration.

18. To Mrs. Richard F. Cary, June 3, 1864, and Feb. 9, 1865, in Edwina Booth

Grossman, *Edwin Booth: Recollections by His Daughter* (1894; rpt. New York: Benjamin Blom, 1969), pp. 27-28.

19. The promptbooks, press reports, and other records of this lavish production are surveyed in John Ripley, *Julius Caesar on Stage in England and America, 1599-1973* (Cambridge, Eng.: Cambridge University Press, 1980), pp. 115-39. Its outstanding features seem to have been its spectacular sets and Booth's successful feat of acting three major roles (Brutus, Cassius, and Mark Antony) in succession during the run of 103 nights.

20. *HEB*, p. 68; Grossman, pp. 15-16.

21. Quoted in *HEB*, pp. 70-71.

22. Shattuck has reproduced Charles Witham's watercolors from a souvenir promptbook of 1870; see *HEB*, pp. 107-9 and plates 4-9. This promptbook is now preserved in the Harvard Theatre Collection, which acquired it in 1965. The effects of Booth's Theatre are described and illustrated in O. B. Bunce, "Behind, Below, and Above the Scenes," *Appleton's Journal*, 3 (May 28, 1870), 589-94.

23. See criticisms by Nym Crinkle and O.B. Bunce, quoted in *HEB*, pp. 91-93, 287; Shattuck, *HEB*, p. 50.

24. Quoted in *HEB*, p. 72. This pamphlet is scarce; I have consulted copies in the Folger Shakespeare Library and the Harvard Theatre Collection.

25. Lawrence W. Levine, *Highbrow/Lowbrow: The Emergence of Cultural Hierarchy in America* (Cambridge, Mass.: Harvard University Press, 1988), pp. 146, 195.

26. "Nym Crinkle," New York *World*, Jan. 9, 1870, and June 9, 1893.

27. This outline of Clarke's life is derived from *HEB*, pp. 102-4, and Murray Bundy, "A Record of Edwin Booth's *Hamlet*," *Shakespeare Quarterly*, 2 (1951), 99-102. Apparently, a fuller account of his life and writings once existed but has now disappeared. Emma Clarke, his daughter, offered two biographical sketches to the Folger Library, but they were refused. The Eastern Washington State Historical Society in Spokane has some of Clarke's published stories and western diaries; but it does not have any such biographical outline.

28. Hereafter I will quote directly from Clarke's manuscript, citing the consecutive numbers inscribed over each written column (col. 1 over the memorandum book space for May 2, 1870; col. 2 over the space for May 3; and so on). For his purposes, Shattuck does not cite in this way but sometimes quotes, sometimes paraphrases, and sometimes conflates Clarke with other sources.

29. Daniel J. Watermeier, "Edwin Booth's Performances: New Documentation," *Theatre History Studies*, 2 (1981), 125-28; Daniel J. Watermeier, ed., *Edwin Booth's Performances: The Mary Isabella Stone Commentaries* (Ann Arbor: UMI Research Press, 1989), pp. 144-47.

30. Hamlin Garland, "Edwin Booth as Hamlet" (typescript preserved in the Garland papers in the library of the University of Southern California), p. 41.

31. See Edwin M. Royle, "Edwin Booth as I Knew Him," *Harper's Magazine* (1916), and a review by Nym Crinkle, both quoted in Lockridge, pp. 302-4. Booth's ruinous effect on small community theaters is discussed with some financial figures by Milton Nobles in "The Booth-Barrett Tour," New York *Dramatic Mirror* (June 2, 1888), quoted in Kimmel, p. 319.

32. Henry A. Clapp, "Edwin Booth," in *Famous American Actors of To-day*, ed. Frederick Edward McKay and Charles E. L. Wingate (New York: Crowell, 1896), p. 50.

33. Edward H. Sothern, *The Melancholy Tale of "Me"* (New York: Scribner, 1918), p. 333.

Chapter 8: Ave atque Vale

1. *The Book of Abigail and John: Selected Letters of the Adams Family 1762-1784*, ed. L. H. Butterfield, Marc Friedlaender, and Mary-Jo Kline (Cambridge, Mass.: Harvard University Press, 1975), pp. 121-23. The blank space appears in John Adams's original letter.

2. John Adams to James Sullivan, May 26, 1776, in *The Works of John Adams*, ed. Charles Francis Adams, 10 vols. (Boston, 1850-56), 10: 377-78.

3. As late as 1945 President Truman's mother balked at the idea she might have to sleep there: "You tell Harry, if he puts me in the room with Lincoln's bed in it I'll sleep on the floor." Truman explains that his family still nursed hard feelings about the Civil War and had resented his blue uniform when he joined the National Guard. See Harry S. Truman, *Memoirs 1: Year of Decisions* (New York: Doubleday, 1955), p. 220.

4. I quote the Latin text from the Loeb Classical Library volume *Catullus, Tibullus and Pervigilium Veneris*, rev. ed. (Cambridge, Mass.: Harvard University Press; London: Heinemann, 1962), p. 172.

Index

A Note on the Author

ALBERT FURTWANGLER is professor of English at Mount Allison University in Sackville, New Brunswick. He is the author of *American Silhouettes: Rhetorical Identities of the Founders* and *The Authority of Publius: A Reading of the Federalist Papers*.